A MISOGYNIST'S SOURCE BOOK

Fidelis Morgan

JONATHAN CAPE
THIRTY-TWO BEDFORD SQUARE LONDON

Ladies and Baggage

Sign over the back entrance of a London club,
cited in a letter to *The Times* 1964

First published 1989
© Fidelis Morgan 1989

Jonathan Cape Ltd, 32 Bedford Square, London WC1B 3SG

A CIP catalogue record for this book
is available from the British Library

ISBN 0-224-02567-8

Phototypeset by Computape (Pickering) Ltd, North Yorkshire
Printed in Great Britain by
Mackays of Chatham PLC, Chatham, Kent

Contents

Contents

Foreword

Extract from *The Wife of Bath's Prologue* by
Geoffrey Chaucer

    At the month's end,
This jolly cleric, Jenkyn, that was so hende [gay],
Hath wedded me with great solemnity;
And to him gave I all the land and fee [property]
That ever was me given therebefore.
But afterward repented me full sore;
He nolde suffer nothing of my list [He wouldn't let me
    have my own way].
By God! he smote me one on the lyst [ear],
For that [because] I rent out of his book a leaf,
That of the stroke my ear wax all deaf.
Stibourn [fierce] I was as is a lioness,
And of my tongue a very jangleress [chatterbox],
And walk I would, as I had done before,
From house to house, although he had it sworn
    [forbidden];
For which he often-times would preach,
And me of old Roman geestes [stories] teach;
How he Symplicius Gallus left his wife,
And her forsook for term of all his life,
Nought but for open-headed he her saw
Looking out at his door upon a day.
    Another Roman told he me by name,

That, for his wife was at a summer's game
Without his witting, he forsook her eke.
And then would he upon his Bible seek
That ilke [same] proverb of Ecclesiaste
Where he commandeth, and forbiddeth fast,
Man shall not suffer his wife go roule [gad] about.
Then he would say right thus, without a doubt:
  'Whoso that buildeth his house all of sallows,
And pricketh his blind horse over the fallows,
And suff'reth his wife to go seeking hallows [shrines],
Is worthy to been hanged on the gallows!'
But all for nought, I settle nought an haw,
Of his proverbs n'of his old saw [I thought nothing of his
  sayings],
Nor I would not of him corrected be.
I hate him that my vices telleth me,
And so do more, God wot, of us than I.
This made him with me wood all outrely [flaming mad],
I nolde nought forbear him in no cas [I wouldn't give him
  any peace].
  Now will I say you sooth, by Saint Thomas,
Why that I rent out of his book a leaf,
For which he smote me so that I was deaf.
  He had a book that gladly, night and day,
For his desport he would read alway;
He cleped [called] it Valerie and Theofraste [Valerius and
  Theophrastus],
At which book he laughed always full fast.
And eke there was sometime a cleric at Rome,
A cardinal, that hight [was called] Saint Jerome,
That made a book against Jovinian;
In which book eke there was Tertulan [Tertullian],
Crisippus, Trotula, and Heloise,
That was abbess not far from Paris;
And eke the Parables of Solomon,
Ovid's Art, and books many on,
And all these were bounden in one volume.

And every night and day was his custom,
When he had leisure and vacation
From other worldly occupation,
To read on this book of wicked wives.
He knew of him more legends and lives
Than been of good wives in the Bible.
For trusteth well, it is an impossible
That any cleric will speak good of wives,
But if it be of holy saints' lives,
Nor of none other woman never the more.
Who painted the lion, tell me who?
By God! if women had written stories,
As clerics have within their oratories,
They would have written of men more wickedness
Than all the mark of Adam may redress . . .
The clerick, when he is old, and may nought do
Of Venus' works worth his old shoe,
Then sits he down, and writes in his dotage
That women can not keep her marriage!

  But now to purpose, why I told thee
That I was beaten for a book, pardee!
Upon a night Jenkyn, that was our sire [husband],
Read on his book, as he sat by the fire,
Of Eva first, that for her wickedness
Was all mankind brought to wretchedness,
For which that Jesu Christ himself was slain,
That bought us with his heart blood again.
Lo, here express of woman may ye find,
That woman was the loss of all mankind.

  Then read he me how Samson lost his hairs:
Sleeping, his leman [girlfriend] cut it with her shears;
Through which treason lost he both his eyes.

  Then read he me, if that I shall not lie,
Of Hercules and of his Deianire,
That caused him to sette himself afire.

  No thing forgot he the care and the woe
That Socrates had with his wives two;

How Xantippa cast piss upon his head.
This silly man sat still as he were dead;
He wiped his head, no more does he seyn [say],
But 'Ere that thunder stint, cometh a rain!'
    Of Pasiphae, that was the Queen of Crete,
For shrewdness, him thought the tale sweet;
Fie! speak no more — it is a grisly thing —
Of her horrible lust and her liking.
    Of Clytemnestra, for her lechery,
That falsly made her husband for to die,
He read it with full good devotion.
    He told me eke for what occasion
Amphiaraus at Thebes lost his life.
My husband had a legend of his wife,
Eriphyle, that for a brooch of gold
Hath privately unto the Greeks told
Where that her husband hid him in a place,
For which he had at Thebes sorry grace.
    Of Lyvia told he me, and of Lucy:
They both made their husbands for to die;
That one for love, that other was for hate,
Lyvia her husband, on an even' late,
Empoisoned hath, for that she was his foe;
Lucia, lecherous, loved her husband so
That, for he should always upon her think,
She gave him such a manere [powerful] love-drink
That he was dead ere it were by the morrow;
And thus allgates [every way] husbands have sorrow.
    Then told he me how one Latumius
Complained unto his fellow Arrius
That in his garden growed such a tree
On which he said how that his wives three
Hanged themselves for herte despitus [for spite],
'O leif [dear] brother,' quoth this Arrius,
'Give me a plant of this blessed tree,
And in my garden planted shall it be.'
    Of latter date, of wives hath he read

That some have slain their husbands in their bed,
And let their lecher dighte [sleep with] her all the night,
When that the corpse lay in the floor upright.
And some have driven nails in their brain,
While that they slept, and thus they have him slain.
Some have him gave poison in their drink.
He spoke more harm than heart may bethink;
And therewithal he knew of more proverbs
Than in this world there grows grass or herbs.
'Better is,' quoth he, 'thy habitation
Be with a lion or a foul dragon,
Than with a woman using for to chide [used to chiding].'
'Better is,' quoth he, 'he in the roof abide,
Than with an angry wife down in the house;
They been so wicked and contrarious,
They hate that their husbands love ay [anything].'
He said, 'A woman casts her shame away,
When she casts off her smock;' and furthermore,
'A fair woman, but she be chaste also,
Is like a gold ring in a sow's nose.'
Who would wene [believe], or who would suppose,
The woe that in my heart was, and pyne [torment]?
    And when I saw he would never fyne [finish]
To read on this cursed book all night,
All suddenly three leaves have I plyght [plucked]
Out of his book, right as he read, and eke
I with my fist so took him on the cheek
That in our fire he fell backwards a-down.
And he up started as doth a wood lion,
And with his fist he smote me on the head,
That in the floor I lay as I were dead.
And when he saw how still that I lay,
He was aghast, and would have fled his way,
Till at last out of my swogh I breyde [recovered from my
    swoon].
'O! hast thou slain me, false thief?' I said,
'And for my land thus hast thou murdered me?

Ere I be dead, yet will I kiss thee.'
  And near he came, and kneeled fair a-down,
And said, 'Dear sister Alisoun,
As help me God! I shall thee never smite.
That I have done, it is thyself to wit [You're to blame for
  what I've done].
Forgive it me, and that I thee beseech!'
And yet eftsoones [again] I hit him on the cheek,
And said, 'Thief, thus much am I wreke [avenged];
Now will I die, I may no longer speak.'
But at last, with much care and woe,
We fille acorded by us selven two [We made it up with
  one another].
He gave me all the bridle in my hand,
To have the governance of house and land,
And of his tongue, and of his hand also;
And made him burn his book anon right tho [there and
  then].

Introduction

A collection of misogynist quotes is not a new idea. The Wife of Bath's husband, Jenkyn, had one in the fourteenth century. No doubt the book discussed by Chaucer was not the first of its type in existence and it was certainly not the last (there was for instance a glut of these books in the 1960s, classed as 'humorous stocking-fillers for male chauvinist pigs'].

Jenkyn's book, like its modern equivalents, was directed at the misogynist market, to bolster bruised egos in the wake of female emancipation, to salve itchy consciences and to give respectable precedents for inexcusable behaviour, like wife-beating and rape.

A Misogynist's Source Book is intended for *everyone*, particularly for all the people who were not supposed to read those earlier books.

I decided to make a collection of anti-woman quotes while researching my first book *The Female Wits*, when I had daily to plough through anti-woman comment parading itself as fact to get to the *real* facts beneath.

I did not start collecting until a few years later, and my initial intention was to collect quotes from sources universally considered the pillars of our society.

I started in The British Library, using the reference books on the open shelves: religious tracts, law textbooks, medical books, encyclopaedias, dictionaries, and classics of world literature; thence to the Official Publications Library for Acts of Parliament, parliamentary advisory papers, law reports, journals of the House of Commons and *The Times* Index.

Then, one evening while scrubbing a floor prior to polishing it, I put on a record of Beatles' songs which had come out when I was twelve. I remembered gaily singing these songs with my schoolfriends while strumming our tennis racquets. That night twenty years later I sang along again as I scrubbed.

> I'd rather see you dead little girl
> Than to be with another man . . .
> You'd better run for your life if you can, little girl,
> Hide your head in the sand, little girl,
> Catch you with another man,
> That's the end, little girl.

As I sang I heard the words as though for the first time. What surprised me was the casualness of the violence expressed over such a jaunty tune.

It occurred to me that this song, and many others like it, was a descendant of the things I had been pulling from the reference shelves, and I realised that the attitudes displayed by all the major religious texts were not so different from the views expressed from the dock of The Old Bailey by murderers of women. The voice of God heard by the Yorkshire Ripper in the Bingley cemetery is an example of extravagant overkill, for there are enough passages in the Bible to work anybody up into a deadly fear and loathing of women.

My collection now expanded to include snippets from popular culture. I flicked at random through magazines, newspapers, songbooks, I watched television, went to the cinema and the theatre, jotting down as I went. Within weeks my collection ranged from Buddhist tracts to the Beatles, from the Bard of Avon to the Boston Strangler.

Night after night as I collected I reeled home from The British Library. As time went by, so my reactions to the material I was amassing altered. I started in a calm, knowing astonishment, but this rapidly declined into anger, frustration, disgust and misery. I went through a strange period of being as disappointed when I did not come home with any juicy quotes as I was when I did. The disappointment, though, took contrasting forms: the first was disappointment with myself, the second with everyone else.

For a few days I actually found myself starting to believe the things I read, and then I began to ignore some pretty outrageous quotes only because they seemed so reasonable in comparison with the rest. This was the most shocking proof of the power of propaganda. I could see that if continual subjection to this sort of thing over a period of weeks could put doubts into *my* head, then, over the centuries, the steady trickle of misogyny must have a sure effect on the relative confidence of women and the people who believe women to be inferior.

Men, of course, are not the only misogynists, for, as Thackeray put it, 'to be despised by her sex is a very great compliment to a woman' and conversely the women who do the despising also manage to make themselves seem more glamorous – two great female wits of the eighteenth century, Madame de Stael and Lady Mary Wortley Montagu, are included within this book.

I set myself a quite arbitrary deadline and called a halt to collecting that day. I then tried to find some sort of order within my collection. I showed the whole thing to friends, to see their responses.

I was asked by some whether it would not be possible to compile a book about hatred of men. The answer is yes . . . *but*: it could not have such a catholic selection, such a scan of history, and it would not include so many great literary figures, or so many apparently reasonable and wise people.

Some asked whether certain quotes weren't in reality balanced by their male equivalents. I have not set out in this book to make any attempt at a comparative study of the treatment of men and women. However, to give one example, here is Roget's Thesaurus entry on women:

> **woman**, Eve, she; petticoat, skirt; girl, virgin, maiden
> 895n., ma'am *spinster*; co-ed, undergraduette;
> lady; bride, matron 894n. *spouse*; mother 169n.
> *parent*; wench, lass, nymph; dame 537n. *teacher*;
> blonde, brunette; sweetheart, bird 887n. *loved one*;
> moll, doll, broad, mistress 952n. *loose woman*;
> quean; shrew, virago, Amazon.

This amazing collection of women has obviously passed a
different entrance qualification to the following band of
merry men:

> **man**, he; virility, manliness, masculinity, manhood;
> mannishness, viraginity, gynandry; he-man,
> cave-m; gentleman, sir, esquire 870n. *title*; wight,
> fellow, guy, blade, bloke, beau, chap, cove, card,
> chappie, johnny, buffer; gaffer, goodman, male
> relation 11n. *kinsman*, 169n, parent 132n. *young-
> ster*, 170n. sonship, 894n. spouse; bachelor; stag
> party, menfolk.

No mention at all of the rats, cads, bounders and bastards
who feature so strongly in this book – fictional heroes and
anti-heroes as well as real life rotters.

From Oedipus through Hamlet to Jimmy Porter, play-
wrights, poets, songwriters and novelists have let their
leading men open their mouths and pour out torrents of
abuse against women whose lives they have made a misery.

Of course it is the poet's job to reflect life as it is, not
how it might be, and it is important not to confuse author
with characters. I do not wish anyone to assume that
if an author is quoted in this book that that author is a
woman-hater. While misogyny provides such a strong
undercurrent in society, writers of fiction *must* continue
to include misogynist characters. For instance, Desiderius Erasmus in *In Praise of Folly* gives his anti-women
speeches to a perfect fool. I have quoted from this character, and many like him, because he is the beautifully

honed voice of misogyny through the ages – even though Erasmus's use of that voice was certainly ironic.

My younger sister was cross to find a quote by her hero, John Keats. 'He had good reason to loathe women,' she said. 'His girlfriend was horrid to him.' Reason enough, I agree, to be horrid about his girlfriend, but not about womankind. The nineteenth-century French philosopher Remy de Gourmont admitted, 'Most men who rail against women are railing against one woman only.' I may have included people who have excuses for the things they have said about women, but the rights and wrongs of their cases must be discussed elsewhere.

I would like to point out that many of my own heroes are here in a fairly inexcusable light – John Wilmot, Earl of Rochester, and le Duc de la Rochefoucauld, for example. Equally, many well-known misogynists have escaped, simply because I did not chance upon them while collecting.

I have kept as much as possible to quotations which do express generalised ill-feeling towards women. Occasionally, though, I have included criticism directed against an individual, because that individual represents a general tendency within a very specific field. Two examples are the scientist Rosalind Franklin, whose scientific genius was doubted because she didn't wear lipstick or mix'n'match clothing, and Queen Elizabeth I, a petticoat ruler.

I have also included people who said one thing one day and the opposite the next. At thirty they may have hated women, at fifty adored them. For me, the quotes made at thirty count, for, as I have said before, it is not the misogyny of an individual which interests me but the sentiment itself.

A remarkable comment on the power of misogynist literature came from a devoutly Christian man who I noticed averting his eyes when he saw any quote which was taken from the Bible. He told me he had been quite shocked when, early in the manuscript, he read a biblical quote, and was frightened that if he read too many of them he would lose his faith.

Introduction

My friend's personal censorship was his own decision, and not one made for him by a government or local council. I would like to make it very clear that I do not want misogynist literature removed from anyone's bookshelves. There are appalling moves afoot to remove 'sexist' books from public libraries and to stop performing plays which display 'stereotypical attitudes to women'. Hitler banned books, Stalin prohibited plays, and both learned that hiding unpalatable things from public view does not make them go away. Fleas swept under a carpet will merely multiply. Sweep them out into the light and you can deal with them.

True, the Wife of Bath dealt with her husband by making him burn his misogynist omnibus, but not before giving him a very bad shock and making him face up to the ultimate expression of his own misogyny – her murder, albeit feigned.

Note: The arrangement of the text

The quotations in this book are divided into sections based on different attitudes to and thoughts about Woman.

Within each section the overall concept is pursued, backwards, forwards and sideways, through its many variations, in a format similar to a traditional thesaurus of words and phrases.

There seemed more point in organising the quotations in this way because:

1   It should help the reader to locate, within each section, a number of quotations similar in content but different in source.
2   It demonstrates parallels in attitude, across time and culture.
3   It shows how an innocuous statement can develop, Chinese-whispers style, into something altogether more dangerous.
4   It exposes some pretty strange bedfellows.

There is an alphabetical list of authors and sources at the back of the book.

Beginning

Adam and Lilith never found peace together; for when he wished to lie with her, she took offence at the recumbent posture he demanded. 'Why must I lie beneath you?' she asked. 'I also was made from dust, and am therefore your equal.' But Adam tried to make her obedient to him by force. And Lilith, in a rage, uttered the magic name of God, rose into the air and left him.

Numera Rabba (medieval Midrash on Adam's first wife, Lilith – Eve was his third)

*A*ll *daughters of Eve*

And the Lord God caused a deep sleep to fall upon Adam,
and he slept: and He took one of his ribs, and closed up the
flesh instead thereof; And the rib, which the Lord God had
taken from man, made He woman.

'Genesis', *Holy Bible* (Judaeo-Christian text)

woman, Eve, she; petticoat, skirt; girl, virgin, maiden
895n., ma'am *spinster*; co-ed, undergraduette; lady; bride,
matron 894n. *spouse*; mother 169n. *parent*; wench, lass,
nymph; dame 537n. *teacher*; blonde, brunette; sweetheart,
bird 887n. *loved one*; moll, doll, broad, mistress 952n.
loose woman; quean; shrew, virago, Amazon.

Roget's Thesaurus 1975

> When Eve upon the first of men
> The apple pressed with specious cant,
> Oh, what a thousand pities then
> That Adam was not adamant.

THOMAS HOOD 1799–1845
'A Reflection'

And do you know that you are Eve? God's sentence hangs
over all your sex and His punishment weighs down upon
you. You are the devil's gateway; it was you who first

violated the forbidden tree and broke God's law. You coaxed your way around man whom the devil had not the force to attack. With what ease you shattered that image of God: man! Because of the death you deserved, the Son of God had to die. And yet you think of nothing but covering your gowns with jewellery? You should always go in mourning and rags.

TERTULLIAN *c.* A.D. 160–225
De Culta Feminarum

In today's world it is the women and not the men who are doing all the seducing ... Reality shows us that the real seducers are the daughters of Eve who sashay their way through God's world with their mini-skirts, low-cut and see-through blouses and tight-tight pants, for the sole purpose of exhibiting their curvaceous bodies to attract the attention and eyes of men.

JUDGE EMERSON PEREIA
Brazil 1975

It was Adam that was created first, and Eve later, nor was it Adam that went astray; woman was led astray, and was involved in transgression. Yet woman will find her salvation in child-bearing, if she will but remain true to faith and love and holy living.

'St Paul to Timothy I', *Holy Bible* (Christian text)

My research indicates that Eve was the ideal woman. She knew her place. She did not even keep a kitchen girl.

DAVID ROSS LOCKE 1833–88
'Woman's Place'

Adam was led to sin by Eve and not Eve by Adam. It is just and right that woman accept as lord and master him whom she led to sin.

ST AMBROSE c. A.D. 340–97

Whilst Adam slept, Eve from his side arose:
Strange his first sleep should be his last repose.

The Consequence (anon.)

Woman's authority is nil; let her in all things be subject to the rule of man ... And neither can she teach nor be a witness, nor give a guarantee, nor sit in judgement. Adam was beguiled by Eve, not she by him. It is right that he whom woman led into wrongdoing should have her under his direction, so that he may not fail a second time through female levity.

The Body of Canon Law

Adam was lucky – Eve could never nag him about all the other men she could have married.

Joke

Act kindly towards women, for they were created from a rib and the most crooked part of a rib is its top. If you attempt to straighten it you will break it, if you leave it alone it will remain crooked: so act kindly towards women.

'Kitab al-jami as-sahih', al Bukhari (Islamic text)

The woman was not taken
From Adam's head, we know,
To show she must not rule him –
'Tis evidently so.

All daughters of Eve

The woman she was taken
From under Adam's arm,
So she must be protected
From injuries and harm.

ABRAHAM LINCOLN 1809–65
'Adam and Eve's Wedding Song'

Creating from the rib is a metaphorical expression which signifies the stubbornness generally found in the temperament of women and that is due to their physique, psychological set-up of their mind and the nature of the work assigned to them. Women are physically weaker than men; they cannot therefore defend and protect themselves with their physical strength. Nature by bestowing upon them two qualities, stubbornness and shyness, has equipped them for their own protection and safeguard of their individualities.

MUHAMMAD IMRAN
Ideal women in Islam 1979

You see, dear, it is not true that woman was made from man's rib; she was really made from his funny bone.

J.M. BARRIE 1860–1937
What Every Woman Knows

Adam knew perfectly well that the words of the serpent were contrary to the words of God. Yet he wished to eat the fruit against his own conscience, so as not to annoy or anger his rib, his flesh, Eve. He would have preferred not to have done it. But when he was more obedient to his wife than to God, he lost his understanding of good and evil, so that he could not wish nor choose anything good.

BALTASAR HÜBMAIER d. 1528
On Free Will

Oh! why did God,
Creator wise, that peopled highest Heaven
With Spirits masculine, create at last
This novelty on Earth, this fair defect
Of Nature?

JOHN MILTON 1608–74
Paradise Lost

Were there no women, men might live like gods.

THOMAS DEKKER c. 1570–1641
The Honest Whore

Ah, wasteful woman, she who may
On her sweet self set her own price,
Knowing man cannot choose but pay,
How has she cheapen'd Paradise;
How given for nought her priceless gift,
How spoil'd the bread and spill'd the wine,
Which, spent with due respective thrift,
Had made brutes men and men divine.

COVENTRY PATMORE 1823–96
The Angel in the House

Women do many things, just because they are forbidden,
from which they would refrain were it not forbidden. God
knows, these same thistles and thorns are inborn in them!
Women of this kind are children of mother Eve, who
flouted the first prohibition. Our Lord God gave Eve the
freedom to do as she pleased with fruits, flowers, and
grasses, and with all that there was in Paradise – excepting
one thing, which he forbade her on pain of death. Priests
tell us that it was the fig-tree. She broke off its fruit and
broke God's commandment, losing herself and God. But
indeed it is my firm belief today that Eve would never have

done so, had it never been forbidden her. In the first thing she ever did, she proved true to her nature and did what she was forbidden! But as good judges will all agree, Eve might well have denied herself just that one fruit. When all is said and done, she had all the rest at her pleasure without exception, yet she wanted none but that one thing in which she devoured her honour! Thus they are all daughters of Eve who are formed in Eve's image after her.

GOTTFRIED VON STRASSBURG *c.* 1200
Tristan

God created woman. And boredom did indeed cease from that moment – but many other things ceased as well! Woman was God's second mistake.

F.W. NIETZSCHE 1844–1900
The Antichrist

I wish Adam had died with all his ribs in his body.

DION BOUCICAULT 1822–90

A perfect woman

Who among women is the best? The Holy Prophet replied:
She who gives pleasure to him [her husband] when he
looks, obeys him when he bids and who does not oppose
him regarding herself and her riches, fearing his dis-
pleasure.

'Kitab as-sunan', *al Nasai* (Islamic text)

Hey, little girl, comb your hair, fix your make-up –
Soon he will open the door.
Don't think because there's a ring on your finger
You needn't try any more.
For wives should always be lovers too.
Run to his arms the moment he comes home to you.
I'm warning you.

Day after day there are girls at the office,
And men will always be men.
Don't send him off with your hair still in curlers,
You may not see him again,
For wives should always be lovers too,
Run to his arms the moment he comes home to you.
He's almost here.

Hey, little girl, better wear something pretty,
Something you'd wear to go to the city;
And dim all the lights, pour the wine, start the music,
Time to get ready for love.

14

A perfect woman

Oh, time to get ready, time to get ready,
Time to get ready for love.

HAL DAVID
'Wives and Lovers' 1963

That moment she was mine, mine, fair,
Perfectly pure and good: I found
A thing to do, and all her hair
In one long yellow string I wound
Three times her little throat around,
And strangled her. No pain felt she;
I am quite sure she felt no pain.
As a shut bud that holds a bee
I warily oped her lids; again
Laughed the blue eyes without a stain.

ROBERT BROWNING 1812–89
'Porphyria's Lover'

It is the highest and eternal duty of women – namely, to
sacrifice their lives and to seek the good of their husbands.

'Adī Parva', *Mahābhārata* (Hindu text)

Try this text for a week. Starting tonight determine that you
will admire your husband. By an act of will, determine to
fill up his cup, which may be bone dry. Be positive.
Remember that compliments will encourage him to talk.
Admire him as he talks to you. Concentrate on what he's
saying. Let him know you care. Put your magazine down
and look at him. Even if you don't care who's won
yesterday's football game, your attention is important to
him and he needs you. Let him know he's your hero.

MARABEL MORGAN
The Total Woman 1973

To most men the attractive and desirable thing in a woman is not outward beauty but winsomeness of manner and action.

Fascinating Womanhood, Psychology Press 1930

What most men desire is a virgin who is a whore.

EDWARD DAHLBERG
Reasons of the Heart 1965

The ten properties of a woman:
Ye.i.is to be merry of chere, ye.ii.to be wel placed, ye.iii. to haue a broad forhed, ye.iiii.to haue brod buttocks, ye.v.to be hard of ward, ye.vi.to be easy to leap upon, ye.vii.to be good at long iourney, ye.viii.to be wel sturring under a man, ye.ix.to be always busy wt ye mouth, ye.x.euer to be chewing on ye bridle.

Fitzherbert's Boke of Husbandry 1568

She was totally female, obedient to her passionate cruel woman's temperament; active and alive, the more refined the more savage and the more hateful the more exquisite.

JORIS-KARL HUYSMANS 1848–1907
À Rebours

A perfect woman, nobly planned,
To warn, to comfort, and command,
And yet a spirit still, and bright,
With something of angelic light.

WILLIAM WORDSWORTH 1770–1850
'She Was a Phantom of Delight'

A perfect woman

Got myself a crying, talking,
Sleeping, walking,
Living doll.

LIONEL BART 1959
– sung by Cliff Richard

A wife domestic, good and pure
Like snail should keep within her door;
But not like snail, in silver track
Place all her wealth upon her back.
A woman should like echo true
Speak but when she's spoken to;
But not like echo still be heard
Contending for the final word.
Like a town clock a wife should be
Keep time and regularity;
But not like clocks harangue so clear
That all the town her voice might hear.

18th-century street ballad

A man who has found a vigorous wife has found a rare
treasure, brought from distant shores.
Bound to her in loving confidence, he will have no need of
spoil.
Content, not sorrow, she will bring him as long as life
lasts.
Does she not busy herself with wool and thread, plying her
hands with ready skill?
Ever she steers her course like some merchant ship, bringing
provision from far away.
From early dawn she is up, assigning food to the household,
so that each waiting woman has her share.
Ground must be examined, and bought, and planted out as
a vineyard, with the earnings of her toil.

How briskly she girds herself to the task, how tireless are her arms!

Industry, she knows, is well rewarded, and all night long her lamp does not go out.

Jealously she sets her hand to work, her fingers clutch the spindle.

Kindly is her welcome to the poor, her purse ever open to those in need.

Let the snow lie cold if it will, she has no fears for her household; no servant of hers but is warmly clad.

Made by her own hands was the coverlet on the bed, the clothes of lawn and purple that she wears.

None so honoured at the city gate as that husband of hers, when he sits in council with the elders of the land.

Often she will sell linen of her own weaving, or make a girdle for the travelling merchant to buy.

Protected by her own industry and good repute, she greets the morrow with a smile.

Ripe wisdom governs her speech, but it is kindly instruction she gives.

She keeps watch over all that goes on in her house, not content to go through life eating and sleeping.

That is why her children are the first to call her blessed, her husband is loud in her praise:

Unrivalled art thou among all the women that have enriched their homes.

Vain are the winning ways, beauty is a snare; it is the woman who fears the Lord that will achieve renown.

Work such as hers claims its reward; let her life be spoken of with praise at the city gates.

'Proverbs', *Holy Bible* (Judaeo-Christian text)

This, then, I believe to be, – will you not admit it to be? – the woman's true place and power. But do not you see that, to fulfil this, she must – as far as one can use such terms of a human creature – be incapable of error? So far as she rules, all must be right, or nothing is. She must be enduringly, incorruptibly good; instinctively, infallibly wise – wise not for self-development, but for self-renunciation: wise, not that she may set herself above her husband, but that she may never fail from his side: wise, not with the narrowness of insolent and loveless pride, but with the passionate gentleness of an infinitely variable, because infinitely applicable, modesty of service – the true changefulness of woman.

JOHN RUSKIN 1819–1900
Sesame and Lilies

If a Wagogo hunter is unsuccessful, or is attacked by a lion, he attributes it to his wife's misbehaviour at home, and returns to her in great wrath. While he is away hunting, she may not let any one pass behind her or stand in front of her as she sits; and she must lie on her face in bed.

J.G. FRAZER 1854–1941
The Golden Bough

Since thou'rt condemn'd to wed a thing,
And that same thing must be a she,
And that same she to thee must cling
For term of life of her and thee,
I'll tell thee what this thing shall be.

I would not have her virtuous,
For such a wife I ne'er did see,
And 'tis a madness to suppose
What never was, nor e'er shall be.
To seem so is enough to thee.

Do not desire she should be wise,
Yet let her have a waggish wit;
No circumventing subtleties,

But pretty slights to please and hit,
And make us laugh at her, or it.

Nor must thou have one very just,
Lest she repay thee in thy kind,
And yet she must be true to trust;
Or if to sport she has a mind,
Let her be sure to keep thee blind.

One part of valour let her have,
Not to return but suffer ill.
To her own passion be no slave,
But to thy laws obedient still,
And unto thine submit her will.

Be thou content she have a tongue
That's active so it be not loud,
And so she be straight-limbed and young,
Though not with beauty much endow'd;
No matter, so she be but proud.

Tired she should be, not satisfied,
But always tempting thee for more,
So cunningly she been't espied;
Let her act all parts like a whore,
So she been't one, I'd ask no more.

But above all things, let her be
Short lived and rich, no strong-dock'd Jone,
That dares to live till fifty-three.
Find this wife, if thou must have one,
But there's no wife so good as none.

ALEXANDER BROME 1620–66

'A Wife'
The ideal wife is a beautiful, sex-starved deaf-mute who owns a liquor store.

More Playboy's Party Jokes 1965

A perfect woman

As a general rule, a modest woman seldom desires any sexual gratification for herself. She submits to her husband, but only to please him; and, but for the desire of maternity, would far rather be relieved from his attention. No nervous or feeble young man need therefore be deterred from marriage by an exaggerated notion of the duties required from him.

DR WILLIAM ACTON 1814–75
The Function and Disorders of the
Reproductive Organs

The perfect woman has a brilliant brain, wants to make love until four in the morning – and then turns into a pizza.

DAVID LEE ROTH 1988

The dream of the American male is for a female who has an essential langour which is not laziness, who is unaccompanied except by himself, and who does not let him down. He desires a beautiful, but comprehensible, creature who does not destroy a perfect situation by forming a complete sentence.

E.B. WHITE 1899–1985
'Notes on our time'

Wife wanted:
Must be able to
Look like an Angel
Cook like a gourmet
And bonk like a rabbit.

T-shirt 1988

Being married to those sleepy-souled women is just like playing at cards for nothing: no passion is excited and the time is filled up. I do not, however, envy a fellow one of those honeysuckle wives for my part, as they are but creepers at best and commonly destroy the thing they so tenderly cling about.

SAMUEL JOHNSON 1709–84

A virtuous wife rules

In the family the wife has her full substantive place, and in the feeling of family piety realises her ethical disposition.

GEORG HEGEL 1770–1831
The Philosophy of Right

A virtuous wife rules her husband by obeying him.

PUBLIUS SYRUS 1st century B.C.
Opinions

The married woman is a slave whom one must be able to set on a throne.

HONORÉ DE BALZAC 1799–1850
The Physiology of Marriage

She who ne'er answers till a husband cools,
Or, if she rules him, never shows the rules;
Charms by accepting, by submitting sways,
Yet has her humour most, when she obeys.

ALEXANDER POPE 1688–1744
'Epistle to a Lady'

Though destitute of virtue or seeking pleasure elsewhere, or devoid of good qualities, a husband must be constantly worshipped as a god.

Laws of Manu (Hindu text)

Wives must obey their husbands as they would obey the Lord.

'St Paul to the Ephesians', *Holy Bible* (Christian text)

The subordination of wife to husband is natural, but above all it is in obedience to God's divine plan.

PROFESSOR J.M.V. BROWNER
Vive la Difference 1984

The husband is the ruler of the family and the head of the wife, the woman as flesh of his flesh and bone of his bone is to be subordinate and obedient to a husband not, however, as a handmaid but as a companion of such a kind that the obedience given is as honourable as dignified. As, however, the husband ruling represents the image of Christ and the wife obedient the image of the Church, Divine love should at all times set the standard of duty.

POPE LEO XIII 1878–1903
Arcanum Encyclical

It's a woman's duty to obey her husband ... my admiration for women is very much bound up with their beauty and grace. I am constantly appalled by the strident voices of women claiming equality with men.

PROFESSOR C. NORTHCOTE PARKINSON 1909–88

A woman's virtue may be easily described: her virtue is to order her house, and keep what is indoors, and obey her husband.

PLATO 427–347 B.C.
Meno

It is our pleasure that no woman, on account of her own depraved desires, shall be permitted to send a notice of divorce to her husband on trumped-up grounds; as, for instance, that he is a drunkard or a gambler or a philanderer, nor indeed shall a husband be allowed to divorce his wife on every sort of pretext. But when a woman sends a notice of divorce, the following criminal charges only shall be investigated, that is, if she should prove that her husband is a homicide, a sorcerer, or a destroyer of tombs, so that the wife may thus earn commendation and at length recover her entire dowry.

Theodosian Code A.D. 331

Be a good husband aged, infirm, deformed, debauched, offensive, a drunkard, a gambler, a frequenter of places of ill repute, living in open sin with other women, and destitute of honour, still a wife should regard him as a god.

Padma Purāna (Hindu text)

But what if a man of lewd and beastly conditions, as a drunkard, a glutton, a profane swaggerer, an impious swearer and blasphemer, be married to a wise, sober, religious matron, must she account him her superior and worthy of an husband's honour? Surely she must. For the evil quality and disposition of his heart and life doth not deprive a man of that civil honour which God hath given unto him.

WILLIAM GOUGE
Of Domesticall Duties 1634

The sight and touch of a chaste woman who always eats the refuse of the food of her husband, and drinks water with which his feet are washed, are desired always by the gods.

'Krishna Janma-Khanda', *Brahma-Vaivarta*
(Hindu text)

Three times every day, at dawn, midday prayer and evening prayer, they stand back in the presence of their own husband and fold their arms and speak thus: "What are thy thoughts so that I may think them; what is necessary for thee that I may speak it; and what is necessary for thee so that I may do it?"

For any command and whatever the husband orders it is requisite to go about that day.

Sad Dar (Zoroastrian text)

It is only when a woman surrenders her life to her husband, reveres and worships him, and is willing to serve him, that she becomes really beautiful to him. She becomes a priceless jewel, the glory of femininity, his queen!

MARABEL MORGAN
The Total Woman 1973

A good housewife is of necessity a humbug.

WILLIAM MAKEPEACE THACKERAY 1811–63
Vanity Fair

A *virtuous wife rules*

The cloy of all pleasure, the luggage of life,
Is the best that can be said for a very good wife.

JOHN WILMOT, EARL OF ROCHESTER, 1647–80
'On a Wife'

A man can bear anything but the mention of his wives.

Arabian proverb

Trouble and strife – wife.

Cockney rhyming slang

A woman who frowns at her husband, or abuses him, goes
to the hell of meteors, and dwells there for as many years as
the hairs on his body.

'Prakriti-Khanda', *Brahma-Vaivarta* (Hindu text)

A woman who annoys her husband with her tongue, she
incurs the reproach and wrath of Allah, all the angels and
the human beings.

Hazrat Abu Bakr (Islamic text)

The woman whose life is of the head will strive to inspire
her husband with indifference; the woman whose life is of
the heart, with hatred; the passionate woman, with disgust.

HONORÉ DE BALZAC 1799–1850
The Physiology of Marriage

The bed that contains a wife is always hot with quarrels
And mutual bickering: sleep's the last thing you get there.
This is her battleground, her station for husband-baiting:
In bed she's worse than a tigress robbed of its young,

Bitching away, to stifle her own bad conscience,
About his boy-friends, or weeping over some way-out
Fictitious mistress. She keeps a copious flow
Of tears at the ready, awaiting her command
For any situation: and you, poor worm, are agog,
Thinking this means she loves you, and kiss her tears
    away.
But if you raided her desk-drawers, the compromising
    letters,
The assignations you'd find that your green-eyed whorish
Wife has amassed!

JUVENAL *c.* A.D. 55–140
Satires

When a man marries it is no more than a sign that the
feminine talent for persuasion and intimidation . . . has
forced him into a more or less abhorrent compromise with
his own honest inclinations and best interests.

H.L. MENCKEN 1880–1956
'The War Between Man and Woman'

There are few wives so perfect as not to give their husbands
at least once a day good reason to repent of ever having
married, or at least of envying those who are unmarried.

JEAN DE LA BRUYÈRE 1645–96
Characters

Was she worth it? – bingo use: 76: from former price of UK
marriage licence, 7/6.

JONATHON GREEN
The Dictionary of Contemporary Slang 1984

A fair wife without a fortune is a fine house without furniture.

THOMAS FULLER 1608–61
Gnomologia no. 481

Well dowered wives bring evil and loss to their husbands.

PLAUTUS *c.* 250–184 B.C.
Aulularia

He that has lost a wife and sixpence has lost sixpence.

Scottish proverb

But now my kitten's grown a cat,
And cross like other wives,
Oh! by my soul, my honest Mat,
I fear she has nine lives.

JAMES BOSWELL 1740–95
Convivial song

God save us all from wives who are angels in the street, saints in the church, and devils at home.

CHARLES HADDON SPURGEON (Baptist preacher)
1834–92
John Ploughman's Talk

Man has found remedies against all poisonous creatures, but none was yet found against a bad wife.

FRANÇOIS RABELAIS *c.* 1494–1553
Works IV

What rugged ways attend the noon of life!
Our sun declines, and with what anxious strife,
What pain, we tug that galling load, a wife!

WILLIAM CONGREVE 1670–1729
The Old Bachelor

HUSBAND PUT WIFE IN 'ELECTRIC CHAIR'
An abandoned husband tried to kill his cheating wife by
attaching her to a homemade electric chair.

Roy Crombleholme choked her into unconsciousness,
connected bare wires to her fingers and switched on the
supply.

Susan Crombleholme, 30 and a mother-of-two, survived
but had to have two fingers amputated . . .

As Crombleholme sobbed in the dock his wife, who is
still living with lover Michael Hulme, told the judge: 'He
obviously didn't realise what he was doing.'

Daily Mail 1988

There was a little pretty lad
And he lived by himself,
And all the meat he got
He put upon a shelf.

The rats and the mice
Did lead him such a life
That he went to Ireland
To get himself a wife.

The lanes they were so broad
And the fields they were so narrow,
He couldn't get his wife home
Without a wheelbarrow.

The wheelbarrow broke,
My wife she got a kick.

A virtuous wife rules

The deuce take the wheelbarrow
That spared my wife's neck.

Nursery rhyme

Perantalu – India, ethn. In Tamilnadu, title given to wives who died before their husband, thus considered as "good spirits".

Encyclopaedia of Asian Civilisations ed. Louis Frederic

A woman whose husband is pleased with her at the time of her death goes straight to Paradise.

'Jami as-sahih', *Abu 'Isa Muhanmad al-Tirmidhi*
(Islamic text)

Here lies my wife: here let her lie!
Now she's at rest, and so am I.

JOHN DRYDEN 1631–1700
Epitaph intended for Dryden's wife

I married the wife of my dreams. Ever since she's been a nightmare.

Joke

31

A *woman and a whisk-broom can accomplish so darn much*

There's a new gadget you can screw on the bed and it does all the housework – your wife.

Joke

A woman's place is in the home looking after the family, not out working.

POPE JOHN PAUL II 1981

Women who work are much more likely to wander than those who don't.

PIERS PAUL READ 1983

The best thing a woman can do is to marry, have children and bring them up herself.

JUDGE DAME ELIZABETH LANE
Speech at Malvern Girl's College 1980

The woman who rejects pregnancy, marriage, make-up and femininity for reasons of health, abandons her natural role in life under these coercive conditions of health. The woman who rejects marriage, pregnancy or motherhood etc. because of work, abandons her natural role under the same coercive conditions. The woman who rejects marriage, pregnancy or maternity etc. without any concrete cause, abandons her natural role as a result of a coercive condition which is a moral deviation from the norm ... Consequently, there must be a world revolution which puts an end to all materialistic conditions hindering woman from performing her natural role in life and driving her to carry out man's duties in order to be equal in rights.

PRESIDENT GADAFFI
The Green Book III 1979

The fact of the matter is that the prime responsibility of a woman probably is to be on earth long enough to find the best mate possible for herself, and conceive children who will improve the species.

NORMAN MAILER
The Presidential Papers 1963

For nothing lovelier can be found
In woman, than to study household good
And good works in her husband to promote.

JOHN MILTON 1608–74
Paradise Lost

HOUSEKEEPING: The care and maintenance of a home includes: (1) providing sufficient and suitable food for all members of the household; (2) care and cleaning of the house, its equipment and furnishings; (3) care and cleaning of the clothing of household members; (4) personal care of members of the family, including care of children and invalids; (5) responsibility for heating and lighting the house and sometimes for its repair; (6) control of household expenditures; (7) engaging and supervising household employees; (8) purchasing food, supplies, equipment, furnishings and clothings; (9) maintaining relations with other families and with organisations in the community; (10) taking part in and sponsoring such civic activities of the community as garbage disposal, water supply, good markets inspection, street cleaning, smoke and dust elimination, or any community housekeeping projects which have bearing on personal housekeeping problems; and (11) making suitable provision for the comfort of family members and guests. Housekeeping is one of the most comprehensive occupations that a woman can undertake.

Encyclopaedia Britannica 1961

A society in which women are taught anything at all but the management of a family, the care of men and the creation of the future generation is a society which is on the way out.

L. RON HUBBARD (founder of Scientology)
Questions for Our Time 1980

A wife made to order can't compare with a ready maid.

Joke

Men marry, indeed, so as to get a manager for the house, to solace weariness, to banish solitude; but a faithful slave is a far better manager, more submissive to the master, more observant of his ways, than a wife who thinks she proves herself mistress if she acts in opposition to her husband, that is, if she does what pleases her, not what she is commanded.

H.L. MENCKEN 1880–1956
'In Defence of Women'

A civil servant of "impeccable character" strangled his wife during an argument over where she put the mustard . . . Later he allegedly told police "it was her fault. I always placed my newspaper on one side of the plate and mustard on the other. But she moved my paper and put the mustard in its place."

Daily Mail 1987

The Jew has stolen woman from us through the forms of sex democracy. We, the youth, must march out to kill the dragon so that we may again attain the most holy thing in the world, the woman as maid and servant.

GOTTFRIED FEDER
'The German Woman in the Third Reich' 1932

Everybody ought to have a maid;
Everybody ought to have a working girl,
Everybody ought to have a lurking girl . . .
Everybody ought to have a maid;
Everybody ought to have a menial,
Consistently congenial
And quieter than a mouse . . .

Fluttering up the stairway,
Shuttering up the windows,
Cluttering up the bedrooms,
Buttering up the master . . .

Oh, oh, wouldn't she be delightful,
Sweeping out, sleeping in . . .

Everybody ought to have a maid,
Someone who's efficient and reliable,
Obedient and pliable
And quieter than a mouse . . .

Everybody ought to have a maid;
Someone who's as busy as a bumble bee,
And even if you grumble be
As grateful as a grouse;

Wriggling in the anteroom,
Tickling in the dining room,
Giggling in the living room,
Wiggling in the other rooms,
Pottering all around the house.

STEPHEN SONDHEIM
– from *A Funny Thing Happened on the Way
to the Forum*

They have a right to work wherever they want to – as long
as they have dinner ready when you get home.

JOHN WAYNE 1907–79

I have always thought that there is no more fruitful source
of family discontent than a housewife's badly cooked
dinners and untidy ways. Men are so well-served out of
doors – in their well-ordered taverns and dining-places –
that in order to compete with the attractions of these places
a mistress must be thoroughly acquainted with the theory
and practice of cookery as well as be perfectly conversant
with all the other arts of making and keeping a comfortable
home.

MRS BEETON
Preface to *Household Management* 1861

A woman's touch can weave a spell –
The kind of hocus-pocus that she does so well.
With the magic of a broom
She can mesmerise a room.

With a whisk whisk here
And a whisk whisk there
And a dustpan for the cinders,
With a rub rub here

And a rub rub there
She can polish up the winders . . .
It makes you blink
To stop and think:
A woman and a whisk-broom
Can accomplish so darn much –
So never underestimate a woman's touch.

P.F. WEBSTER & SAMMY FAIN
– from *Calamity Jane* 1954

'Lastly, there is a wife who is like a maid-servant. She serves her husband well and with fidelity. She respects him, obeys his commands, has no wishes of her own, no ill-feeling, no resentment, and always tries to make him happy.'

The Blessed One asked, 'Sujata, which type of wife are you like or would you wish to be like?'

Hearing these words of the Blessed One, she was ashamed of her past conduct and replied that she would wish to be like the one in the last example, the maid-servant. She changed her behaviour and became her husband's helper, and together they sought Enlightenment.

BUKKYO DENDO KYOKAI
The Teachings of Buddha (The Buddhist Promoting
Foundation) 262nd revised edition 1982

Wife: a darning attachment for the domestic machine.

OLIVER HERFORD
Cupid's Cyclopaedia 1910

It takes a woman, all powdered and pink
To joyously clean out the drain in the sink.
And it takes an angel with long golden lashes
And soft Dresden fingers for dumping the ashes.

A Misogynist's Source Book

Yes, it takes a woman, a dainty woman,
A sweetheart, a mistress, a wife.
Oh yes it takes a woman, a fragile woman,
To bring you the sweet things in life.

JERRY HERMAN
– from *Hello Dolly* 1964

But men's shadows

Woman is a stupid vessel over whom man must always hold power, for the man is higher and better than she; for the regiment and dominion belong to man as the head and master of the house; as St Paul says elsewhere: man is god's honour and god's image.

Item: Man does not exist for the sake of woman, but woman exists for the sake of the man and hence there shall be this difference that a man shall love his wife, but never be subject to her, but the wife shall honour and fear the husband.

MARTIN LUTHER 1483–1546
Vindication of Married Life

Woman is a miserable creature, always inferior to man, less handsome than he, less ingenious, less wise, disgustingly shaped, the opposite of what could please man or delight him.

MARQUIS DE SADE 1740–1814
Justine

The female sex is in some respects inferior to the male sex, both as regards body and soul.

The Catholic Encyclopaedia ed. C.G. Herbermann 1907

You are quite right in maintaining the general inferiority of the female sex; at the same time many women are in many things superior to many men, though speaking generally what you say is true.

PLATO 427–347 B.C.
Republic

Woman is the lesser man, and all thy passions match'd
  with mine,
Are as moonlight unto sunlight, and as water unto wine.

ALFRED, LORD TENNYSON 1809–92
'Locksley Hall'

Virtuous women wisely understand
That they were born to base humility.

EDMUND SPENSER *c.* 1552–99
The Faerie Queene

Bitter indeed it is to be born a woman.
It is difficult to imagine anything so low!

FU HSUAN
Yu-t'-ai-hsin-yung

I love men, not because they are men but because they are not women.

QUEEN CHRISTINA (of Sweden) 1626–89

I thank God I am not a woman, to be touched with so many giddy offences as he hath generally taxed their whole sex withal.

WILLIAM SHAKESPEARE 1564–1616
As You Like It

I am glad that I am not a man, as I should be obliged to marry a woman.

MADAME DE STAËL 1766–1817

Women have no existence and no essence; they are not, they are nothing. Mankind occurs as male or female, as something or nothing . . . The meaning of woman is to be meaningless. She represents negation, the opposite pole from the Godhead, the other possibility of humanity.

OTTO WEININGER (philosopher who influenced Nazi movement)
Sex and Character 1906

Blessed art thou O Lord our God, King of the Universe, who has not made me a woman.

Daily prayer for Jewish males

> If the tenth too is a girl child
> I will cut both of your feet off,
> Both your arms up to the shoulders;
> Both your eyes, too, I will put out.
> Blind and crippled you will be then,
> Pretty little wife, young woman.

Bulgarian folksong

If we could guarantee a boy I'd definitely get pregnant.

RULA LENSKA 1987

The sonless can never go to the heavens; so he must get a son somehow or other.

Devī Bhāgavata (Hindu text)

41

When any one of them has tidings of a female child, his face is overclouded and black, and he has to keep back his wrath. He skulks away from the public for the evil tidings he has heard: is he to keep it in disgrace, or to bury it in the dust?

Surah (Islamic text)

ABORTION OF "WRONG SEX" BABY GIRLS
Doctors are breaking the law to abort healthy babies because their parents want boys and not girls claims a report out today.

Glasgow Herald 1988

On the tenth day from conception pains in the head, giddiness and dim sight, distaste for food, and vomiting are symptoms of the formation of the embryo. If the child is a male, the mother has a better colour and an easier delivery; there is movement in the womb on the fortieth day. In a case of the other sex all the symptoms are the opposite: the burden is hard to carry, there is a slight swelling of the legs and groin, but the first movement is on the ninetieth day.

PLINY A.D. 23–79
Natural History

Do you think it's going to be a boy . . . or a child?

TERRY WOGAN
– to Anna Ford, BBC TV 1985

You see my dear, my beauty, that I have hateful prejudices about women. In fact, I have no faith; you have a fine soul, but, when all is said, it is the soul of a woman . . . a few days ago you were a deity, which is so convenient, so noble, so inviolable. And now there you are, a woman.

CHARLES PIERRE BAUDELAIRE 1821–67
Letter to Apollone Sabatier

In her particular nature, woman is defective and mis-begotten, for the active force in the male seed tends to the production of a perfect likeness in the masculine sex; while the production of woman is due to a weakness in the generative force or imperfection in the pre-existing matter or even from some external influences, for example the humid winds from the south.

ST THOMAS AQUINAS 1225–74
Summa Theologica

The people of Darfur, in Central Africa, think that the liver is the seat of the soul, and that a man may enlarge his soul by eating the liver of an animal . . . Women are not allowed to eat liver, because they have no soul.

J.G. FRAZER 1854–1941
The Golden Bough

I believe in the natural superiority of man as I believe in the existence of God.

CAROLINE NORTON (poet and novelist) 1808–77

The weaker sex, to piety more prone.

SIR WILLIAM ALEXANDER *c.* 1567–1640
'The Fifth Hour', *Doomsday*

In every excellent character, whether mental or physical, the average woman is inferior to the average man, in the

43

sense of having that character less in quantity and lower in quality . . . Even in physical beauty man is superior.

T.H. HUXLEY 1825–95

> If I was with a woman
> I'd threaten to unload her
> Every time she asked me to explain.
> If I was with a woman
> She'd have to learn to cherish
> The purity and depth of my disdain.

IAN DURY
'If I Was With a Woman' 1979

The female is more imperfect than the male. The first reason is that she is colder. If, among animals, the warmer ones are more active, it follows that the colder ones must be more imperfect . . . Just as man is the most perfect of all animals, so also, within the human species, man is more perfect than woman. The cause of this superiority is the [male's] super-abundance of warmth, heat being the primary instrument of nature . . .

GALEN *c*. A.D. 130–201
Works

In passing out from the great gate (of her father's house) he precedes, and she follows, and with this the right relation between husband and wife commences. The woman follows (and obeys) the men: in her youth, she follows her father and elder brother; when married, she follows her husband; when her husband is dead, she follows her son.

Kıâo Theh Săng (Chinese text)

The male precedes and the female follows; the husband precedes and the wife follows. The precedence of the more honourable and sequence of the meaner is seen in the action of heaven and earth and hence the sages took them as their pattern.

Kwang Tze (Taoist text)

There is no objection to women members of pious associations and Catholic Action taking part with lighted candles in Catholic liturgical processions, provided they march after the celebrant and the proper order be observed so that the more worthy associations march nearer to the celebrant.

'Sacred Processions: participation by women'
Canon Law 1933

As a recommended caution, a woman must stand behind a man and the place of her prostration be located a little behind that of the man.

AYATOLLAH KHOMEINI
A Clarification of Questions 1980

I asked a Burmese why women, after centuries of following their men, now walk ahead. He said there were many unexploded land mines since the war.

ROBERT MUELLER

Pig's knuckles, clear beetroot soup and other Polish delights will await Pope John Paul II for his first dinner in Mexico, and nuns at an apostolic residence will taste the food first as a security measure.

United Press International article 1979

Therefore God's universal Law
Gave to the man despotic power
Over his female in due awe,
Nor from that right to part an hour,
Smile she or lour;
So shall he least confusion draw
On his whole life, not sway'd
By female usurpation, nor dismay'd

JOHN MILTON 1608–74
Samson Agonistes

An employment agency survey shows that out of 500 male office workers 25% would not take a job when their boss would be a woman.

Daily Express 1981

For to make woman our superior in all the qualities proper to her sex, and to make her our equal in all the rest, what is this but to transfer to the woman the superiority which nature has given to her husband?

JEAN-JACQUES ROUSSEAU 1712–78
Émile

I adore you, ladies, but you are not my equal.

ANTHONY QUINN 1983

Descent to or through a daughter, however, normally takes place after all the sons (and their issue and descendants) are exhausted, irrespective of whether the daughter was born before or after her brothers.

PATRICK MONTAGUE-SMITH (of Debrett)
The Royal Line of Succession 1953

It is annoying and impossible to suffer proud women, because in general Nature has given men proud and high spirits, while it has made women humble in character and submissive, more apt for delicate things than for ruling.

BOCCACCIO 1313–75
'Niobe', *Concerning Famous Women*

Women feel more; sensibility is the power of woman. They often rule more effectually, more sov'reignly, than man. They rule with tender looks, tears and sighs; but not with passion and threats; for if, or when, they so rule, they are no longer women, but abortions.

JOHN CASPAR LAVATER 1741–1801
Essays on Physionomy

Queen Elizabeth had long outlived men's affection if not their fear and respect and after fifty years of petticoat government they welcomed a male ruler, and the end of female tantrums, sulks and irrationality.

J.P. KENYON
Stuart England 1978

Obedience to a woman will have to be repented of.

Arabian proverb

Man is above woman as Christ is above man. It is unchangeable that woman is destined to live under man's influence, and has no authority from her lord.

ST THOMAS AQUINAS 1225–74
Summa Theologica

Dwell not in a country in which there is no law or . . . which is governed by a woman or an infant.

Garuda (Hindu text)

To promote a Woman to bear rule, superiority, dominion, or empire, above to Nature, contumely to God, is a thing most contrarious to his revealed will and approved ordinance; and finally it is the subversion of good Order, of all equity and justice.

JOHN KNOX *c.* 1513–72
*First Blast of the Trumpet against the Monstrous
Regiment of Women*

We have been discussing the possibility of positive discrimination for women and I don't think it is a bad idea. On a committee of six people positive discrimination would mean there should be at least two women.

WILLIAM RODGERS M.P. 1982

And women shall have rights similar to the rights against them according to what is equitable; but men have a degree over them.

Koran (Islamic text)

It will upset the apple-cart if women get equal pay.

Union official at Vauxhall Motors, Luton 1977

Say are not women truly, then,
Styled but the shadows of us men.

BEN JONSON 1572–1637
'That Women are but Men's Shadows'

Chaos, darkness and woman

The Tao: The pure and the turbid, has motion and rest.
Heaven is pure and earth is turbid,
Heaven moves and earth is at rest,
The masculine is pure and the feminine is turbid,
The masculine moves and the feminine is still.

Khing Kang King (Taoist text)

Taimat was a personification of the sea and represented the feminine element which gave birth to the world. In the continuation of the story she represents the blind forces of primitive chaos against which the intelligent and organising gods struggle.

'Assyro-Babylonian mythology', *New Larousse Encyclopaedia of Mythology* 1968

Words are women, deeds are men.

GEORGE HERBERT 1593—1633
Jacula Prudentum

It is not enough even to be able to speak the language of that nation by which they are written, for there is a memorable interval between the spoken and the written language, the language heard and the language read. The one is commonly transitory, a sound, a tongue, a dialect merely,

49

almost brutish, and we learn it unconsciously, like the brutes, of our mothers. The other is the maturity and experience of that; if that is our mother tongue, this is our father tongue, a reserved and select expression, too significant to be heard by the ear, which we must be born again in order to speak.

HENRY DAVID THOREAU 1817–62
Walden

Yang – positive cosmic force, the heavens, man.
Yin – negative cosmic force, earth, woman.

Tung Chung Shu (Confucian text)

There is a good principle, which has created order, light and man; and a bad principle, which has created chaos, darkness and woman.

PYTHAGORAS *c.* 550–500 B.C.

As specific energy, we may say that the libido is a force of virile character. We will say as much of the orgasm.

MARAÑON (a sexologist)

Masturbation, at all events of the clitoris, is a masculine activity and the elimination of the clitoral sexuality is a necessary pre-condition for the development of femininity.

SIGMUND FREUD 1856–1939
'Some Psychological Consequences of the Anatomical Distinctions Between the Sexes'

What is woman? Only one of Nature's agreeable blunders.

HANNAH COWLEY 1743–1809
Who's the Dupe?

Chaos, darkness and woman

The ideal woman is a man, though women lie low and let that secret keep itself.

GEORGE BERNARD SHAW 1856–1950
Letter to Ellen Terry

There is but one thing in the world worse than a shameless woman and that's another woman.

ARISTOPHANES *c.* 450–385 B.C.
Thesmophoriazusae

It goes far to reconcile me to being a woman that I reflect that I am thus in no danger of marrying one.

LADY MARY WORTLEY MONTAGU 1689–1762

I am tempted to think that to be despised by her sex is a very great compliment to a woman.

WILLIAM MAKEPEACE THACKERAY 1811–63
Vanity Fair

That very thought that I am a woman makes my wings droop.

ST THERESA OF AVILA 1515–82

womanish, a. (Of man or his feelings, conduct, looks etc.) like women or their ways etc. (usu. derog.), effeminate.

Concise Oxford English Dictionary

Female as 'a mere synonym for "woman"' is 'now commonly avoided by good writers, except with contemptuous implication' (the OED) or with a facetious one.

Usage and Abusage ed. Eric Partridge 1947

Cigars in the street

In those rare individual cases where women approach genius they also approach masculinity.

WAVERLEY ROOT
'Women are intellectually inferior' 1949

Ye belles, and ye flirts, and ye pert little things,
Who trip in this frolicsome round,
Pray tell me from whence this impertinence springs,
The sexes at once to confound?
What means the cocked hat, and the masculine air,
With each motion designed to perplex?
Bright eyes were intended to languish, not stare,
And softness the test of your sex.

The girl, who on beauty depends for support,
May call every art to her aid;
The bosom displayed, and the petticoat short,
Are samples she gives of her trade.
But you, on whom fortune indulgently smiles,
And whom pride has preserved from the snare,
Should slyly attack us with coyness, and wiles,
Not with open and insolent war.

The Venus, whose statue delights all mankind,
Shrinks modestly back from the view,
And kindly should seem by the artist designed
To serve as a model for you.

Then learn, with her beauty, to copy her air,
Nor venture too much to reveal:
Our fancies will paint what you cover with care,
And double each charm you conceal.

The blushes of morn, and the mildness of May,
Are charms which no art can procure:
O be but yourselves, and our homage we pay,
And your empire is solid and sure.
But if, Amazon-like, you attack your gallants,
And put us in fear of our lives,
You may do very well for sisters and aunts,
But, believe me, you'll never be wives.

WILLIAM WHITEHEAD 1715–85
'Song for Ranelagh'

WILD WOMEN Those who go in for "women's rights" and
general topsyturvyism. Some smoke cigars in the streets,
some wear knickerbockers, some stump the country as
"screaming orators", all try to be as much like men as
possible.
   'Let anyone commend these female runagates quietness,
duty, home-staying, and the whole cohort of wild women is
like an angry beehive, which a rough hand has disturbed'.

Brewer's Dictionary of Phrase & Fable 1978
(first published 19th century)

4: Antifeminine Girls. This group included all the girls in
the sample who said they did not want to marry. These
girls showed psychological deviance and signs of severe
pathology.

DOUVAN & ADELSON
'Patterns of sex identification of high school girls' 1975

The rights of women who demand,
Those women are but few:
The greater part had rather staid
Exactly as they do.

Beauty has claims for which she fights
At ease with winning arms;
The women who want women's rights
Want mostly, women's charms.

Punch 1870

Don't swagger around in public nor attempt to thrust yourself forward. A modest girl will not let herself become prominent in public places. Dressing, acting or talking in any way to attract undue attention will soon ruin a girl's reputation.

WILLIAM LEE HOWARD
Confidential Chats with Girls 1927

Possessed by a restless discontent of their appointed work, and fired with a mad desire to dabble in all things unseemly, which they call ambition; blasphemous to the sweetest virtues of their sex, which until now have been accounted with their own pride and the safeguard of society; holding it no honour to be reticent, unselfish, patient, obedient, but swaggering to the front, ready to try conclusions in aggression, in selfishness, in insolent disregard of duty, in cynical abasement of modesty, with the hardest and least estimable of the men they emulate; these women of the doubtful gender have managed to drop all their own special graces while unable to gather up any of the more valuable virtues of men.

MRS LYNN LINTON 1822–98
The Epicene Sex

Cigars in the street

Give a woman a job and she grows balls.

JACK GELBER

The really original woman is the one who first imitates a man.

ITALO SVEVO 1861–1928
A Life

It is evident that if there is such a tension as penis-envy in certain women, it can never be satisfied directly, and therefore has to be satisfied indirectly by getting something else that boys don't have. The most natural way to do this is by having babies, which, after all, are things boys cannot have; furthermore, a boy can have only one penis, while a woman can have many babies. Some women, however, avoid such feminine acquisitions as babies, and try to beat the man at his own game in order to assuage their envy, which brings them into a business or profession where they will be in direct competition with the opposite sex. If a woman's choice of occupation is based on such penis-envy, she will eventually become unhappy, because she will be frustrating the tension of her physis, which is urging her towards a feminine line of development.

ERIC BERNE
A Layman's Guide to Psychiatry and Psychoanalysis
1969

Women do not find it difficult nowadays to behave like men; but they often find it extremely difficult to behave like gentlemen.

SIR COMPTON MACKENZIE 1883–1972
'On Moral Courage'

Deprive man of his virile member

Some time ago I chanced to have an opportunity of obtaining insight into a dream of a newly-married woman which was recognizable as a reaction to the loss of her virginity. It betrayed spontaneously the woman's wish to castrate her young husband and to keep his penis for herself.

SIGMUND FREUD 1856–1939
'The Taboo of Virginity'

How, as it were, they deprive man of his virile member: We have already shown that they can take away the male organ, not indeed by actually despoiling the human body of it, but by concealing it with some glamour . . . Witches who in this way sometimes collect male organs in great numbers, as many as twenty or thirty members together, and put them in a bird's nest, or shut them up in a box, where they move themselves like living members, and eat oats and corn . . . A certain man tells that, when he had lost his member, he approached a known witch to ask her to restore it to him. She told the afflicted man to climb a certain tree, and that he might take which he liked out of a nest in which there were several members. When he tried to take a big one, the witch said: You must not take that one; adding, because it belonged to a parish priest.

JACOB SPRENGER & HENDRICH KRAMER
Malleus Maleficarum (the indispensable handbook and ultimate authority for the Inquisition) 1489

Deprive man of his virile member

The unsatisfied wish for a penis should be converted into a wish for a child and for a man who possesses a penis.

SIGMUND FREUD 1856–1939
Analysis Terminable and Interminable

Domain of the masculine intellect

Man is the rival of other men; he delights in competition, and this leads to ambition which passes too easily into selfishness. These latter qualities seem to be his natural and unfortunate birthright. It is generally admitted that with woman the powers of intuition, of rapid perception, and perhaps of imitation, are more strongly marked than in man; but some, at least, of these faculties are characteristic of the lower races, and therefore of a past and lower state of civilisation.

CHARLES DARWIN 1809–82
The Descent of Man

[Women] are not aware of the fact that they have paid a high price for it [intellectuality] in their feminine values. Women's intellectuality is to a large extent paid for by the loss of valuable feminine qualities: it feeds on the sap of the affective life and results in impoverishment of this life ... intuition is God's gift to the feminine woman; everything relating to exploration and cognition, all the forms and kinds of human cultural aspiration that require a strictly objective approach are, with few exceptions, the domain of the masculine intellect, of man's spiritual power, against which woman can rarely compete. All observations point to the fact that the intellectual woman is masculinized; in her, warm intuitive knowledge has yielded to cold unproductive thinking.

HELENE DEUTSCH
Psychology of Women I 1946

Women's intuition is the result of millions of years of not thinking.

RUPERT HUGHES 1872–1956

If a woman's intuition's as good as they say, why must they keep asking questions?

Joke

Whimsey, not reason, is the female guide.

GEORGE GRANVILLE 1667–1735
The Vision

Women are generally shy, capricious and whimsical, and are easily carried off by their emotions, and thus their study of the situation is hardly objective.

MUHAMMAD IMRAN
Ideal women in Islam 1979

Woman: with allusion to qualities generally attributed to the female sex, as mutability, capriciousness, proneness to tears; also to their position of inferiority or subjection (phr. to make a woman of, to bring into submission).

Oxford English Dictionary

Women would rather be right than reasonable.

OGDEN NASH 1902–71
'Frailty, Thy Name Is a Misnomer'

I have no other but a woman's reason:
I think him so, because I think him so.

WILLIAM SHAKESPEARE 1564–1616
Two Gentlemen of Verona

We use to say, it's a woman's reason to say, I will do such a thing, because I will do it.

JEREMIAH BURROUGHS 1599–1646
On Hosea

There can be no logic in a woman's mind or heart unless it is abetted by her disposition.

LA ROCHEFOUCAULD 1613–80
Maxims

A woman cannot grasp that one must act from principle; as she has no continuity she does not experience the necessity for logical support of her mental processes . . . she may be regarded as 'logically insane'.

OTTO WEININGER
Sex and Character 1906

Exhibit the logical form for the following sentences by translating them into the notation of the predicate calculus: (a) Susan is featherbrained; (b) Janet is featherbrained; (d) All women are featherbrained; (f) No man is featherbrained; (g) Some men are not featherbrained; (h) John is not featherbrained.

Beginning Logic 1982

Domestic chores

The idea that a woman is just as suitable as a man for doing all tasks is ridiculous.

SIR RONALD BELL M.P.
House of Commons 1975

Woman
1 n. female human being (distinguished from man).
2 An adult female person (dist. fr. girl).
3 A mistress or paramour.
4 A female servant, esp. one who does domestic chores, as cleaning, cooking, etc.
5 (formerly) a female personal maid.
6 Feminine nature, characteristics or feelings.
7 A wife.
8 Kept woman; a girl or woman maintained as a mistress by one man.
9 Old woman; a man who is pedantic or tends to fuss, gossip, etc.
10 Scarlet woman; a prostitute, a woman whose sexual relations with a man are considered scandalous.
11 Obs. to cause to act or be like a woman; make effeminate, adj.
12 female: a woman doctor . . .

Macquarie Australian Dictionary

We consider first that the promiscuous assemblage of the sexes in the same class is a dangerous innovation likely to lead to results of an unpleasant character ... That the presence of young females as passive spectators in the operating theatre is an outrage to our natural instincts and feelings and calculated to destroy those sentiments of respect and admiration with which the opposite sex is regarded by all right minded men, such feelings being a mark of civilization and refinement.

> Minutes of a meeting of the medical school committee
> of the Middlesex Hospital, 1861

It is impossible that a woman whose hands reek of gore can be possessed of the same nature as the generality of women.

> Newspaper report of Dr Elizabeth Blackwell's visit
> to London, 1859

Women are certainly capable of learning, but they are not made for the higher forms of science, such as philosophy and certain types of artistic creativity; these require a universal ingredient. Women may hit on good ideas and they may, of course, have taste and elegance, but they lack the talent for the ideal.

> GEORG HEGEL 1770–1831
> *The Philosophy of Right*

The wish to get the longed-for penis eventually in spite of everything may contribute to the motives that drive a mature woman to analysis, and what she may reasonably expect from analysis – a capacity, for instance, to carry on an intellectual profession – may often be recognized as a sublimated modification of this repressed wish.

> SIGMUND FREUD 1856–1939

Let the woman learn in silence, with all subjection. But I suffer not a woman to teach, nor to use authority over the man; but to be in silence.

'St Peter I', *Holy Bible* (Christian text)

The woman taught once, and ruined all. On this account . . . let her not teach. But what is it to other women that she suffered this? It certainly concerns them; for the sex is weak and fickle.

ST JOHN CHRYSOSTOM ('Golden Mouth') c. A.D. 347–407

As the fairest, daintiest natural thing will not brook rough handling or too close and continued examination, the iridescence of the butterfly's wing, the velvet of the rose petal, so the rare and exquisite essence of womanliness will not bear the heat, the mud, the profanation of the public arena.

MR JUSTICE BEAMAN
A paper read to a Ladies' Circle, 1908

Woman is under man's dominion and has no authority, nor can she teach, give evidence, make a contract nor be a judge.

BALTASAR GRACIAN (a Spanish Jesuit) 1601–58

One man who is free from covetousness may be a witness; but not even many pure women, because the understanding of females is apt to waver.

Laws of Manu (Hindu text)

For women should be approached only in private and then with difficulty, not freely and without restraint. Certainly, to allow them as witnesses opens the way to deplorable licence. By bringing them into crowded places, by permitting them to take part in men's affairs, one destroys that submissiveness and modesty which is natural to them and ends up by encouraging brazenness. Moreover, to do this is also, in a certain sense, to wrong men; for what else is it but a wrong, a grievous wrong, to cause the female sex to meddle in matters which pertain uniquely to men?

LEO THE WISE A.D. 886–912

I am opposed to women voting as men vote. I call it immoral, because I think the bringing of one's women, one's mothers and sisters and wives, into the political arena disturbs the relations between the sexes.

HILAIRE BELLOC 1870–1953

The grant of the Parliamentary franchise to women in this country would be a political mistake of a very disastrous kind.

H.H. ASQUITH 1852–1928
Speech at 10 Downing St as Prime Minister

Sensible and responsible women do not want to vote. The relative positions to be assumed by man and woman in the working out of our civilisation were assigned long ago by a higher intelligence than ours.

STEPHEN GROVER CLEVELAND (President of U.S.A.)
1837–1908

Give women the vote, and in five years there will be a crushing tax on bachelors.

GEORGE BERNARD SHAW 1856–1950
Preface to *Man and Superman*

If all women were enfranchised they would at once swamp the votes of men.

SAMUEL EVANS (M.P. for Glamorgan)
House of Commons 1906

Again, if women are suitable for votes, it is impossible to show a single reason why they should not also become Members of Parliament, Cabinet Ministers, Ambassadors, Judges, or indeed, anything else, unless you draw the line at soldiers or sailors.

I, for one, oppose any such revolutionary change of this startling character or a social departure resulting in dangers which no one can foresee.

EARL LOREBURN (Lord Chancellor) 1846–1923

'Man and woman have different spheres assigned to them. To man, nature has given strength and activity, and society has entrusted the right and the duty of protecting and defending his weaker fellow-beings. Man makes and executes laws, administers justice, bears arms, and works for his family. Woman shares in these labours, it is true, but in a subordinate, dependent, and latent manner. Some foolish people have been found who pretended that women had all the rights of men in the administration of things, social and political. Can you fancy a woman – I will not say at the head of a regiment' . . .

'A woman!' laughed Clementina.

'Well a woman could only command women, and you know that Amazons have only existed in mythology, but can you fancy a woman speaking in the courts or the senate, hanging round the ballot box on election day, or sitting in judgement on a criminal?'

'With a lawyer's gown and wig on?' laughed the girls.

Home Education, or a Mother's Advice to her Children,
trans. from the French by Lady Blanche Murphy 1887

The appointment of a woman to office is an innovation for which the public is not prepared. Nor am I.

THOMAS JEFFERSON 1743–1826
Letter to Albert Gallatin

Winston Churchill . . . found a woman's intrusion into the House of Commons as embarrassing as if she had burst upon him in his bathroom when he had nothing to defend himself with but a sponge.

PAMELA BROOKES
Women at Westminster 1967

Life in the House [of Commons] is neither healthy, useful nor appropriate for a woman, and the functions of a mother and a member are not compatible.

MARGOT ASQUITH 1864–1945

A woman in the House of Commons is a contradiction in terms.

ENOCH POWELL M.P. b. 1912

Men and women differ in the same ways as animals and plants. Men and animals correspond just as women and plants do, for women develop in a more static way, keeping the principle of an unspecific unity of feeling or sentiment. When women stand at the head of government, the state is immediately plunged into danger because they conduct affairs not by the standard of universality but in accordance with random opinions and inclinations.

GEORG HEGEL 1770–1831
Foundations of the Philosophy of Right

A nation will never attain success whose control has been entrusted to a woman.

'Kitab al-jami as-sahih', *al Bukhari* (Islamic text)

I consider that women who are authors, lawyers, and politicians are monsters.

PIERRE AUGUSTE RENOIR 1841–1919

She was born to be a creature of sweet impulses – of love – of coquetry – of tenderness – of persuasiveness; and these things, instilled by the unconscious grace and beauty of her natural ways into the spirit of man, are no doubt the true origin of music itself – music which she inspires, but cannot create. It is the same way – to my thinking – with politics ... And woman is not (naturally speaking) a mathematician.

MARIE CORELLI 1855–1924
Woman, or – Suffragette

We have no desire to say anything that might tend to encourage women to embark on accountancy, for although women might make excellent book-keepers there is much in accountancy proper that is, we think, unsuitable for them.

Accountant, English Institute of Chartered Accountants 1912

Courage and magnanimity, such noble accomplishments in man, do very much depress and debase the character of a woman; to whom learning itself is no ornament, but lessens our value of those charms which must be unavoidably either obscured or tarnished by it. The most beautiful woman in the world would not be half so beautiful if she was as great at mathematics as Sir Isaac Newton or as great a metaphysician as the noblest and profoundest school man.

Gentleman's Magazine 1738

A beautiful woman with a brain is like a beautiful woman with a club foot.

BERNARD CORNFIELD 1974

Notwithstanding the enlargement of women's status ... the presumption in law is that she is incapable of understanding a business transaction by the exercise of her own wit.

R.W. JONES
Studies in Practical Banking

There are women, too, among this people of mine who would play the prophetess as their own whim bids them. Turn upon these, son of man, and tell them their doom: Out upon them, says the Lord God.

'Ezechiel', *Holy Bible* (Judaeo-Christian text)

The Five Obstacles:
A woman cannot become a Bonten [King of Brahma Heaven], a Taishaku [Lord God of the Trayastrionsa Heaven], a devil king, a wheel-turning king or a Buddha [enlightened one].

A Dictionary of Buddhist Terms and Concepts
Tomohiro Matsuda (ed.)

And women are to be silent in the churches; utterance is not permitted to them; let them keep their rank, as the law tells them: if they have any question to raise, let them ask their husbands at home. That a woman should make her voice heard in the church is not seemly.

'St Paul to the Corinthians I', *Holy Bible* (Christian text)

Sir, a woman's preaching is like a dog's walking on his hinder legs. It is not done well; but you are surprised to find it done at all.

SAMUEL JOHNSON 1709–84

It is prohibited to any woman to presume to approach the altar or minister to the priest.

Papal decree: Cap Inhibendum I de cohab

Now to get back to the people who don't fly . . . who look upon aviators as some sort of circus trick. I don't think it would surprise them in the least if private pilots turned out to be sword-swallowers and ladies.

H.R.H. PRINCE PHILIP, DUKE OF EDINBURGH
More Wit of Prince Philip 1973

The woman's power is not for rule, not for battle – and her intellect is not for invention or creation, but for sweet orderings, management and decision. She sees the qualities of things, their class, their places.

JOHN RUSKIN 1819–1900
Sesame and Lilies

The incentive for girls to equip themselves for marriage and home-making is genetic.

KATHLEEN OLLERENSHAW
Education for Girls 1961

Physical courage is exclusively a male virtue. Women are constitutionally timid, and their chief virtue is modesty. Any great and unusual exhibition of bravery by a woman, or violent excitement, especially the loud intemperate language of quarrel, with vehement gestures, or manual conflict, almost always causes hysterical reaction, most injurious to health, dangerous, and sometimes fatal: conclusive testimony that woman was never intended to rival man, either in politics or war. The senate, bar, platform, barrack, guardroom and battlefield do not foster womanly virtues.

JAMES McGRIGOR ALLAN
Woman Suffrage Wrong 1890

Most women are mothers, naturally endowed as the best homemakers, and better fitted than men to look after children.

IVOR STANBROOK M.P.
House of Commons 1975

Therefore, women should not be pushed forward or allowed to have prominence in those spheres where Allah has assigned them an inferior position. This is vital for decency and for maintaining equilibrium in the Society; otherwise there will be moral chaos, social imbalance and corruption as is being witnessed today because of the prominence of women in economic, political and social pursuits.

MUHAMMAD IMRAN
Ideal Women in Islam 1979

The Queen is most anxious to enlist everyone who can speak or write to join in checking this mad, wicked folly of "Women's Rights", with all its attendant horrors on which her poor feeble sex is bent, forgetting every sense of womanly feeling and propriety . . . Woman would become the most hateful heartless and disgusting of human beings were she allowed to unsex herself; and where would be the protection which man was intended to give the weaker sex?

QUEEN VICTORIA 1819–1901

A woman's thoughts, beyond the range of her immediate duties, should be directed to the study of men, or the acquirement of that agreeable learning whose sole end is the formation of taste; for the works of genius are beyond her reach, and she has neither the accuracy nor the attention for success in the exact sciences.

JEAN-JACQUES ROUSSEAU 1712–78
Émile

Relationships are important for women. You can't imagine a woman being happy on her own like a man. I just think of marriage and children for girls. There's something sublimated about career women.

STEPHEN SPENDER 1982

Would that there were no woman-myth at all but only a cohort of cooks, matrons, prostitutes, and bluestockings serving functions of pleasure and usefulness.

MICHAEL CARROUGE
Cahiers du Sud, no. 292

All women are good for something or nothing.

Proverb

Women should stick to knitting.

NAPOLEON BONAPARTE 1769–1821

71

Don't seem able to concentrate

Unlike the Amazons, women would be unable to take part in archery or any other skilled use of missiles.

PLATO 427–347 B.C.
Laws

It's not women's bodies that are the problem, it's their minds. They just don't seem able to concentrate as well as men. Which is why they'll never break into the male preserve of championship snooker. Admittedly their shape doesn't help – big breasts can make the game very awkward – but it is that lack of mental control which finally prevents them from becoming top class. Chess is another example – all the best players are men.

STEVE DAVIS 1982

Women's tennis – it's junk – they're robbing men's tennis . . . Men go out and play four or five hard sets. It keeps the crowds on the edge of their seats for three or four hours. And then women go out and play two sets of rubbish which is all over in half an hour . . . most of the girls are no good, there's no depth.

If I played a practice game with Becker when the women's final was on, we'd have more people watching us knock up.

PAT CASH 1987

I would not feel at all happy on the mat myself with a woman refereeing. Many other judo players feel that way.

> DAVID STARBROOK (the British judo team manager
> & Olympic medallist) 1980

There's nothing wrong with the ladies, God bless them; let them play . . . But what they're doing is eliminating much of the available time when young players can get on the course.

> JACK NIKLAUS 1978

When there are ladies present (God bless them!) I walk out on poker. And a fine state of affairs it is when an old newspaperman has to walk out on poker!

> ROBERT BENCHLEY
> 'Ladies Wild'

Poker shouldn't be played in a house with women.

> TENNESSEE WILLIAMS 1911–83
> *A Streetcar Named Desire*

Keith Douglas hit Alison Brewer, 23, with a hammer, stabbed her in the neck and mutilated her body with a knife . . . The computer whizzkid, who butchered his Canadian penpal after she knotched up a fantastic score on a video game, was jailed for life yesterday.

> *Daily Mail* 1987

I was murdered whenever I tried to go on Abbey Brig. And by a woman jockey. They shouldn't be let loose on the race course!

BOB CHAMPION
Champion's Story 1981

The worst time I ever had when I was drunk was when I lost a game of darts – to a woman.

GEORGE BEST 1988

'Football does not come within the Sex Discrimination Act', Lord Denning, Master of the Rolls, ruled in the Court of Appeal yesterday . . . the law was 'an ass and an idiot if it tried to make girls into boys so that they could join in all-boys' games', he said.

The Times 1978

Football is strictly masculine entertainment.

DR NORMAN INLAH (psychiatrist) 1964

A girl of four was bludgeoned to death by her uncle because she switched the TV from a soccer match to cartoons.

Sun 1987

Women are notoriously deficient in sporting blood.

P.G. WODEHOUSE 1881–1975
The Brinkmanship of Galahad Threepwood

Equal rights of *women*

A good woman is worse than a bad man.

Taittiriya Samhita (Hindu text)

To the woman falls the larger share of the work of adjustment: she leaves the initiative to the man and out of her own need renounces originality.

HELENE DEUTSCH
Psychology of Women I 1946

Woman has more wit and man has more genius; woman observes and man reasons.

JEAN-JACQUES ROUSSEAU 1712–78
Letter to D'Alembert

Women represent the triumph of matter over mind, just as men represent the triumph of mind over morals.

OSCAR WILDE 1854–1900
The Picture of Dorian Gray

For her world is her husband, her family, her children and her home. But where would the greater world be if no one cared to tend the smaller world? . . . We do not find it right when the woman presses into the world of the man. Rather

we find it natural when these two worlds remain separate
. . . Woman and man represent two quite different types of
being. Reason is dominant in man. He searches, analyses
and often opens new immeasurable realms. But all things
that he approaches merely by reason are subject to change.
Feeling in contrast is much more stable than reason and
woman is the feeling and therefore the stable element.

ADOLF HITLER 1889–1945
The National Socialist Women's Book

The chief distinction in the intellectual powers of the two
sexes is shewn by man attaining to a higher eminence, in
whatever he takes up, than woman can attain – whether
requiring deep thought, reason, or imagination, or merely
the use of the senses and hands.

CHARLES DARWIN 1809–82
The Descent of Man

Man should be trained for war and woman for the recreation of the warrior; all else is folly.

F.W. NIETZSCHE 1844–1900
Thus spake Zarathustra

Man is the hunter; woman is his game . . .
Man for the field and woman for the hearth:
Man for the sword and for the needle she:
Man with the head and woman with the heart:
Man to command and woman to obey;
All else confusion.

ALFRED, LORD TENNYSON 1809–92
The Princess

Equal rights of women

The whole world was made for man, but the twelfth part of man for woman: man is the whole world and the breath of God; woman the rib and crooked piece of man.

SIR THOMAS BROWNE 1605–82
Religio Medici

But grant in Public Men sometimes are shown,
A Woman's seen in Private life alone:
Our bolder Talents in full light display'd,
Your virtues open fairest in the shade.
Bred to disguise, in Public 'tis you hide;
There, none distinguish 'twixt your Shame or Pride,
Weakness or Delicacy; all so nice
That each may seem a Virtue, or a Vice.
In Men, we various Ruling Passions find;
In Women, two almost divide the kind:
Those, only fix'd, they first or last obey,
The Love of Pleasure, and the love of Sway . . .
Men, some to Bus'ness, some to Pleasure take,
But every Woman is at heart a Rake.
Men, some to Quiet, some to public Strife,
But ev'ry Lady would be Queen for life . . .
And yet, believe me, good as well as ill,
Woman's at best a Contradiction still.

ALEXANDER POPE 1688–1744
'Epistle to a Lady'

Old Man – Good fortune
Old Woman – Scandal

JAMES WARD
Dreams and Omens: Their Meanings c. 1920

Boys will be boys –
And even that . . . wouldn't matter if we could only prevent
girls from being girls.

ANTHONY HOPE 1863–1933
The Dolly Dialogues

And the Lord spoke to Moses, giving him this message for
the Israelites: If a woman conceives, and gives birth to a
boy, she will be unclean for seven days, as she is unclean at
her monthly times. On the eighth day, the child must be
circumcised, and after that she must wait for thirty-three
days more to be purified after her loss of blood, touching
nothing that is hallowed, never entering the sanctuary, until
the time is up. If she gives birth to a girl, she will be unclean
as at her monthly times, for fourteen days, and she will wait
for sixty-six days more to be purified after her loss of blood.

'Leviticus', *Holy Bible* (Judaeo-Christian text)

For indecent assault on a girl aged between 13 and 16 the
maximum penalty is two years' imprisonment. For indecent
assault on a boy under 16 the maximum penalty is 10 years'
imprisonment.

Parliamentary answer to question on paedophilia 1983

He would stand the chance of violent sexual abuse and
becoming a homosexual if sent to a state prison.

JUDGE ROBERT C. ABEL
– explaining the sentence of only 120 days in local jail
for raping and beating a woman, America 1982

Boys are sent out into the world to buffet with its temptations, to mingle with bad and good, to govern and direct
. . . girls are to dwell in quiet homes amongst a few friends,

to exercise a noiseless influence, to be submissive and retiring.

ELIZABETH MISSING SEWELL
'Principle of Education Drawn from Nature and
Revelation and Applied to Female Education in the
Upper Classes' 1865

An evil stepfather wept yesterday after being jailed for 7½ years for raping an 11-year-old who gave birth to his baby ... The man was said at the Old Bailey to have raped his stepdaughter now 13 – six times.

He told her: "Don't tell mum, we don't want to spoil the happiness of the family."

Sun 1988

As unto the bow the cord is,
So unto the man is woman;
Though she bends him, she obeys him,
Though she draws him, yet she follows;
Useless each without the other!

HENRY WADSWORTH LONGFELLOW 1807–82
The Song of Hiawatha

The social presence of a woman is different in kind from that of a man ... A man's presence suggests what he is capable of doing to you or for you ... A woman's presence ... defines what can and cannot be done to her.

JOHN BERGER
Ways of Seeing 1972

A husband could bring an action for the loss of the consortium of his wife by reason of any tort which deprived him of that consortium and in the circumstances prevailing today a wife must have a similar right . . . The Lord Chief Justice, agreeing that the appeal should be dismissed, said that the question that fell for decision might thus be stated: Had a married woman whose husband had been injured by a negligent act or omission a right of action against the person causing the injury for the loss or impairment of consortium consequential on the injury? Mr Justice Croom Johnson in a careful judgement held that no such right existed.

> Best v. Samuel Fox and Co. Ltd, House of Lords,
> *The Times* Law Report 1952

Women represent the interests of the family and the sexual life; the work of civilization has become more and more men's business; it confronts them with ever harder tasks, compels them to sublimations of instinct which women are not easily able to achieve. Since man has not an unlimited amount of mental energy at his disposal, he must accomplish his tasks by distributing his libido to the best advantage. What he employs for cultural purposes he withdraws to a great extent from women, and his sexual life; his constant association with men and his dependence on his relations with them even estrange him from his duties as husband and father.

> SIGMUND FREUD 1856–1939
> *Civilization and its Discontents*

Mr Williams told the court he did not consider it ladylike for women to drink pints in his lounge and said if they wanted to drink like men they should go to the public bar or skittle alley.

> *The Times*, reporting the case of Harold Williams,
> Maltsters Arms, Whitchurch 1980

Equal rights of women

Here is a checklist guide so that you can, with the aid of a
pencil and paper and a spot of arithmetic, work out just
how much food to buy and how far it will go . . .

Meat for casserole .... 6oz per person
Joint with bone .... 6-8oz per person
    "   without bone .... 4–6oz per person
Steak .... 6oz per person
    "   hungry men 8oz

Festive Cooking HP Epicure Pickles

Why can't a woman be more like a man?
Men are so honest, so thoroughly square,
Eternally noble, historically fair.

ALAN JAY LERNER
'A Hymn to Him', *My Fair Lady* 1956

*F*air sex

Whoever it was who first called women the fair sex didn't know much about justice.

More Playboy's Party Jokes 1965

It is only the man whose intellect is clouded by his sexual impulses that could give the name of 'the fair sex' to that undersized, narrow-shouldered, broad-hipped and short-legged race.

ARTUR SCHOPENHAUER 1788–1860
On Women

Men have broad shoulders and narrow hips, and accordingly they possess intelligence. Women have narrow shoulders and broad hips. Women ought to stay at home; the way they were created indicates this, for they have broad hips and a wide fundament to sit upon, keep house, and bear and raise children.

MARTIN LUTHER 1483–1546
Table-talk

When we eliminate women from public life, it is not because we want to dispense with them but because we want to give them back their essential honour ... The outstanding and highest calling of woman is always that of wife and mother, and it would be unthinkable misfortune if we allowed ourselves to be turned from this point of view.

JOSEF GOEBBELS 1897–1945
The National Socialist State

The wave of feminism which swept Britain after 1918 caused widespread unemployment, a general trade depression, and an alarming decline in our birthrate . . . As soon as Hitlerism has been defeated the combined forces of various men's organisations will launch their campaign against a menace just as threatening to Britain as Hitlerism – Feminism.

Leaflet distributed during World War II, by the National Men's Defence League (a British Serviceman's Association) *c.* 1942

The man upholds the nation as the woman upholds the family. The equal rights of woman consist in the fact that in the realm of life determined for her by nature she experiences the high esteem that is her due.

ADOLF HITLER 1889–1945
The National Socialist Women's Book

Femininely meaneth furiously

And femininely meaneth furiously
Because all passions in excess are female.

> GEORGE, LORD BYRON 1788–1824
> *Sardanapalus*

Woman is more compassionate than man, and has a greater propensity to tears, more jealous and querulous, more fond of railing and more contentious.

> ARISTOTLE 384–322 B.C.
> *Historia Animalium*

Women are emotional and an emotional approach is the best approach . . . Reiterate that the prime function in life is to reproduce; that is what God placed her on earth for.

> Training booklet used by the Royal Canadian
> Mounted Police (The Mounties) 1975

How fierce a fiend is passion, with what wildness,
What tyranny untamed, it reigns in woman!
Unhappy sex! Whose easy yielding temper
Gives way to every appetite alike:
Each gust of inclination, uncontrolled,
Sweeps through their soul, and sets them in an uproar;
Each motion of the heart rises to fury,

And love in their weak bosoms is a rage
As terrible as hate, and as destructive.

NICHOLAS ROWE 1674–1718
Jane Shore

Hysteria is a natural phenomenon, the common denomi-
nator of the female nature. It's the big female weapon, and
the test of a man is his ability to cope with it.

TENNESSEE WILLIAMS 1911–83
The Night of the Iguana

Women are of unstable temperament.

Shabbat (Jewish text)

Woman is a creature neither decisive nor constant.

ST AUGUSTINE A.D. 354–430

She is all wavering and hesitation: in short, she is a woman.

JEAN RACINE 1639–99
Athalie

Anthony Clive Lewis, 43, unemployed, of St. Edmund's
Walk, bludgeoned the mother of his two children about the
head with a three-pound hammer and then stabbed her in
the throat, said Mr John Spokes, QC, prosecuting at
Winchester Crown Court.

Moments before the attack Miss Angela James, 26, had
changed her mind "yet again" about moving back to the
mainland, it was stated.

Isle of Wight County Press 1988

Where is the man who has the power and skill
To stem the torrent of a woman's will?
For if she will, she will, you may depend on't;
And if she won't, she won't; so there's an end on't.

> Inscription on a pillar in Canterbury
> cited in the *Examiner* 1829

The female is more dispirited, more despondent, more impudent, and more shameless and false than the male. She is likewise more easily deceived and more apt to remember; and again the female is more watchful, more idle and on the whole less excitable than the male.

> ARISTOTLE 384–22 B.C.
> *Historia Animalium*

Frailty, thy name is woman.

> WILLIAM SHAKESPEARE 1564–1616
> *Hamlet*

Woman: fond, foolish, wanton, flibbergibs, tatlers, triflers, wavering, witless, without counsel, feeble, careless, rash, proud, dainty, nice, talebearers, eavesdroppers, rumour-raisers, evil-tongued, worse-minded and in every wise dultified with the dregs of the devil's dunghill.

> JOHN AYLMER
> *An Harborough for Faithful Subjects* 1559

Woman is more impressionable than man. Therefore in the Golden Age they were better than men; now they are worse.

> COUNT LEO TOLSTOY 1828–1910
> *Diary*

The five worst maladies that afflict the female mind are: indocility, discontent, slander, jealousy and silliness. Without any doubt, these five maladies infest seven or eight out of every ten women, and it is from these that arises the inferiority of women to men. The worst of them all, and the parent of the other four, is silliness. Woman's nature, in comparison with man's, is as the shadow to the sunlight. Hence, as viewed from the standard of man's nature, the foolishness of woman fails to understand the duties that lie before her very eyes, perceives not the actions that will bring down blame upon her own head, and comprehends not even the things that will bring down calamities on the heads of her husband and children. Such is the stupidity of her character that it is incumbent on her, in every particular, to distrust herself and to obey her husband.

EKKEN KAIBARU
The Whole Duty of Women (Japanese rulebook)
c. 1716

A woman is the most heterogeneous compound of obstinate will and self-sacrifice that I have ever met.

JOHANN PAUL FRIEDRICH RICHTER 1763–1825
Flower, Fruit and Thorn Pieces

Every woman is a potential Napoleon, with a possible empire in each successive man she meets.

G. SYDNEY PATERNOSTER
'The Folly of the Wise'

'The gentler sex love blackmail. Show me a delicately nurtured female and I will show you a ruthless Napoleon of crime prepared without turning a hair to put the screws on

87

some unfortunate male whose services she happens to be in need of. There ought to be a law.'

P.G. WODEHOUSE 1881–1975
Jeeves in *Stiff Upper Lip*

All women are fundamentally savage, and the suffragist movement is simply an outbreak of emotional insanity. It is emotional excitement that moves the suffragist to talk at street corners, create disturbances, wrestle with the police.

DR MAX BAFF (Professor of Psychology) 1910

Such is the truth that there is nothing more brutal nor more shameless than a woman.

HOMER *c*. 850–800 B.C.
The Odyssey

All malice is short to the malice of a woman; let the lot of sinners fall upon her. As the climbing of a sandy way is to the feet of the aged, so is a wife full of tongue to a quiet man. Look not upon a woman's beauty, and desire not a woman for beauty. A woman's anger and imprudence, and confusion is great. A woman, if she have superiority, is contrary to her husband. A wicked woman abateth the courage, and maketh a heavy countenance and a wounded heart.

'Ecclesiasticus', *Holy Bible* (Judaeo-Christian text)

The beastly lust, the furious appetite,
The hasty woe, the very great defame,
The blind discretion, and the foul delight
Of womankind that dreads for no shame.

WILLIAM DUNBAR *c*. 1460–1520
'Against Evil Women'

Women are much more like each other than men: they have, in truth, but two passions, vanity and love; these are their universal characteristics.

EARL OF CHESTERFIELD 1694–1773
Letter to his son

All women are born so perverse
No man need boast their love possessing.

ROBERT BRIDGES 1844–1930
'All Women are Born So Perverse'

The Blessed One said, 'Amrapali, the mind of a woman is easily disturbed and misled. She yields to her desires and surrenders to jealousy more easily than a man. Therefore it is more difficult for a woman to follow the Noble Path.'

BUKKYO DENDO KYOKAI
The Teachings of Buddha (The Buddhist Promoting
Foundation) 262nd revised edition 1982

A jealous woman is the grief and mourning of the heart. With a jealous woman is a scourge of the tongue which communicateth with all. As a yoke of oxen that is moved to and fro, so also is a wicked woman: he that hath hold of her is as he that taketh hold of a scorpion. A drunken woman is a great wrath: and her reproach and shame shall not be hid. The fornication of a woman shall be known by the haughtiness of her eyes, and by her eyelids. On a daughter that turneth not away herself, set a strict watch: lest finding an opportunity she abuse herself. Take heed of the impudence of her eyes: and wonder not if she slight thee. She will open her mouth as a thirsty traveller to the fountain and will drink of every water near her, and will sit down by every hedge, and open her quiver against every arrow: until she fail.

'Ecclesiasticus', *Holy Bible* (Judaeo-Christian text)

Since revenge is ever the pleasure of a paltry spirit, a weak and abject mind! Draw this conclusion at once from the fact that no one delights in revenge more than a woman.

JUVENAL *c.* A.D. 55–140
Satires

No fiend in hell can match the fury of a disappointed woman.

COLLEY CIBBER 1671–1757
Love's Last Shift

Sweet is revenge – especially to women.

GEORGE, LORD BYRON 1788–1824
Don Juan

Heav'n has no rage, like love to hatred turn'd,
Nor Hell a fury, like a woman scorn'd.

WILLIAM CONGREVE 1670–1729
The Mourning Bride

Women forgive injuries, but never forget slights.

THOMAS CHANDLER HALIBURTON (Sam Slick) 1796–1865
The Old Judge

She is, also, more envious, more querulous, more slander-ous, and more contentious.

ARISTOTLE 384–322 B.C.
Historia Animalium

Femininely meaneth furiously

Nothing so true as what you once let fall,
"Most Women have no Characters at all".

ALEXANDER POPE 1688–1744
'Epistle to a Lady'

Force

Rape is an act that a man can do but a woman cannot, and
it highlights the differences between men and women . . .
However rape is a perfectly natural function. It means that
a man so desires a woman that he takes her by force. Since
a man is much stronger than a woman it does not necessarily involve much violence, and in many cases the woman
duly submits. Where man and woman are already acquainted what may begin with rape may within a few minutes
turn to loving submission on the part of the woman. In
closer relationships a woman may even like being taken by
force.

PROFESSOR J.M.V. BROWNER 1981
Vive la Difference

Georgie Porgie pudding and pie,
Kissed the girls and made them cry.
When the boys came out to play,
Georgie Porgie ran away.

Nursery rhyme

A woman kissed is half won.

Proverb

Rape . . . is when a man takes a woman sexually by force. Fortunately it is very rare, and even when it does happen it is often because the girl has 'led a man on'.

ANNE ALLEN
The Way You Are: A Handbook for Girls 1963

It is the height of impudence for any girl to hitch-hike at night. That is plain, it isn't really worth stating. She is in the true sense asking for it.

SIR MELFORD STEVENSON Q.C. 1983

For what use woman if not to be taken?

PAUL CLAUDEL 1868–1955
La Cantate à trois voix

The husband cannot be guilty of a rape committed by himself on his lawful wife for by their mutual matrimonial consent and contract the wife hath given herself in this kind unto her husband which she cannot retract.

JUDGE SIR MATTHEW HALE 1609–76
Commentaries on the Laws of England

I kept on raping because at home I wasn't getting enough sex regularly and instead of going without I went out and took it.

DAVE (a convicted rapist)
– in *Why Men Rape* 1980

It is a biologically known fact that in some men abnormal virility is found. If these men are denied polygamy they would certainly inflict cruelty on their spouses and seek in addition illegal sex-gratification outside marriage. This

93

goes to show that man is polygamous by nature and woman is monogamous.

MUHAMMAD IMRAN
Ideal Women in Islam 1979

Higgamous, hoggamous,
Woman's monogamous,
Hoggamous, higgamous,
Man is polygamous.

English rhyme

A little bit of rape is good for man's soul.

NORMAN MAILER
Speech at University of California, Berkeley, 1972

All women may be won.

Proverb

Confucius once say: "If rape is inevitable, relax and enjoy it."

TEX ANTOINE (US WABC-TV weatherman)
– following news report of attempted rape of an
8-year-old girl 1976

A plain skinny spinster with a lisp longed for a man and comforted herself reading the adventures of the ancient gods.

One night she dreamed that a big, blond naked man climbed in through the window, ripped off her nightgown and raped her again and again . . . In the morning when he made to leave she begged him to stay.

"I must return to Valhalla," he shouted. "I'm Thor."

"Tho am I," the spinster laughed, "but wathn't it mar-
vellouth!"

Joke

A maid that laughs is half taken.

Proverb

Every woman loves the idea of a sheikh carrying her off on
his white horse and raping her in his tent. It's a basic
feminine instinct.

OMAR SHARIF
Daily Mail 1981

RAPE AN IRANIAN WOMAN

Placards carried outside the White House in demos
against the Ayatollah Khomeini

It would be much better if young women should stop being
raped much earlier in the proceedings than some of them
do.

MR JUSTICE STABLER 1961

If at first you don't succeed . . . try again she'll be expecting
it.

Joke

Women are like banks, boy. Breaking and entering is a
serious business.

JOE ORTON 1933–67
Entertaining Mr Sloane

I am not saying that a girl hitching home late at night should not be protected by the law, but she was guilty of a great deal of contributory negligence.

JUDGE BERTRAND RICHARDS
Ipswich 1982

Girls also frequently have phantasies of being beaten which later develop into phantasies of being raped. The idea of being forcibly overpowered by a male must have occurred to every woman at some time, although not all women recognise that the apprehension to which such thoughts give rise is not unmixed with pleasure. The situation of being overpowered by a male is also one in which per-mission is given to be erotic, since the victim is forced to comply. Thus she 'cannot help it', and can enjoy the thrill without incurring either blame or responsibility.

ANTHONY STORR
Sexual Deviation 1964

A decent woman must stay at home; the streets are for low women.

MENANDER *c*. 342–292 B.C.

The difference between rape and seduction is only one of technique.

MAGNUS MAGNUSSON
Popular Archaeology 1981

... they slapped her a few times and she mumbled and turned her head but they couldn't revive her so they continued to fuck her as she lay unconscious on the seat in the lot and soon they tired of the dead piece and the daisychain broke up and they went back to Willies the

Greeks and the base and the kids who were watching and waiting to take a turn took out their disappointment on Tralala and tore her clothes to small scraps put out a few cigarettes on her nipples pissed on her jerked off on her jammed a broomstick up her snatch then bored they left her lying amongst the broken bottles rusty cans and rubble of the lot and Jack and Freddy and Ruthy and Annie stumbled into a cab still laughing and they leaned toward the window as they passed the lot and got a good look at Tralala lying naked covered with blood urine and semen and a small blot forming on the seat between her legs as blood seeped from her crotch . . .

HUBERT SELBY
Last Exit to Brooklyn 1966

My son, give me thy heart: and let thy eyes keep my ways. For a harlot is a deep ditch: and a strange woman is a narrow pit. She lieth in wait in the way as a robber: and him, whom she shall see unwary, she will kill.

'Proverbs', *Holy Bible* (Judaeo-Christian text)

Prostitutes are a necessity. Without them men would attack respectable women in the streets.

NAPOLEON BONAPARTE 1769–1821

She wasn't a prostitute but at that time I wasn't bothered, I just wanted to kill a woman.

PETER SUTCLIFFE ('The Yorkshire Ripper')
Old Bailey 1981

Gentle echo

Shepherd: Echo, I ween, will in the wood reply
    And quaintly answer questions: shall I try?
Echo: Try.
S: What must we do our passion to express?
E: Press.
S: How shall I please her, who ne'er loved before?
E: Be fore.
S: What most moves women when we them address?
E: A dress.

S: Say, what can keep her chaste whom I adore?
E: A door.
S: If music softens rocks, love tunes my lyre.
E: Liar.
S: Then teach me, Echo, how shall I come by her?
E: Buy her.
S: When bought, no question I shall be her dear?
E: Her deer.

S: But deer have horns: how must I keep her under?
E: Keep her under.
S: But what can glad me when she's laid on bier?
E: Beer.
S: What must I do when women will be kind?
E: Be kind.
S: What must I do when women will be cross?
E: Be cross.

S: Lord, what is she that can so turn and wind?
E: Wind.
S: If she be wind, what stills her when she blows?
E: Blows.
S: But if she bang again, still should I bang her?
E: Bang her.
S: Is there no way to moderate her anger?
E: Hang her.

S: Thanks, gentle Echo! right thy answers tell
   What woman is and how to guard her well.
E: Guard her well.

JONATHAN SWIFT 1667–1745
'A Gentle Echo on Woman'

Q. What's an echo?
A. An echo is the only thing that can deprive a woman of
   the last word.

Joke

Gongs

A woman, a dog and a walnut tree,
The more you beat them, the better they be.

Proverb

Never skimp the amount of beating. Ices, like women, dogs and walnut trees, are always improved by consistent walloping.

Fanny and Johnny Craddock's Freezer Book

Certain women should be struck regularly, like gongs.

NOEL COWARD 1899–1973
Private Lives

The man has both the right and duty to chastise his girlfriend or wife in certain circumstances. Indeed, it is perfectly natural.

PROFESSOR J.M.V. BROWNER 1981
Vive la Difference

A man having trouble with his rebellious girlfriend goes to his father for advice.

"Well, when your mother started acting up," said the father, "I'd take her knickers down and spank her."

100

"I've tried that," replied his son, "but by the time I get my girl's pants down I'm not angry any more."

Joke

If women got a slap round the face more often, they'd be a bit more reasonable.

CHARLOTTE RAMPLING
Observer 1983

Sweetness, sweetness I was only joking when I said I'd
    like to smash every tooth in your head,
Sweetness, sweetness I was only joking when I said by
    rights you should be bludgeoned in your bed.

MORRISSEY (of The Smiths)
'Big Mouth Strikes Again' 1985

Question: What do mules and women have in common?
Answer: A good beating makes them both better.

Catalonian proverb

I'd rather see you dead, little girl,
Than to be with another man.
You'd better keep your head, little girl,
Or I won't know where I am.

I know that I'm a wicked guy
And I was born with a jealous mind.
And I can't spend my whole life
Tryin' just to make you toe the line.

Let this be a sermon,
I mean ev'ry thing I said.
Baby I'm determined
And I'd rather see you dead.

You'd better run for your life if you can, little girl,
Hide your head in the sand, little girl.
Catch you with another man, that's the end, little girl.

JOHN LENNON & PAUL McCARTNEY
'Run for Your Life' 1965

Directly domineering ceases in the man, snubbing begins in the woman.

THOMAS HARDY 1840–1928
A Pair of Blue Eyes

I did it to scare the lady. I did it because when we were younger we got lots of hits and slaps from women and girls. I did it to scare her.

Twelve-year-old boy who had attacked a woman in a
dark lane, *Western Gazette* 1968

. . . virtuous women, devoted, careful in their husband's absence, as God has cared for them. But those whose perverseness ye fear, admonish them and remove them into bedchambers and beat them.

Koran (Islamic text)

A wife may love a husband who never beats her, but she does not respect him.

Russian proverb

A husband should not insult his wife publicly, at parties. He should insult her in the privacy of the home.

JAMES THURBER 1894–1961
Thurber Country

If a wife refuses to obey and pays no attention to what her husband tells her, it is advisable to beat her with a whip according to the measure of her guilt; but not in the presence of others, rather alone.

> *The Domostroy* (A Russian manual of domestic behaviour) *c.* 1550

A gentleman is someone who raises his hat before he beats his wife.

> Joke

In a number of cases men may be excused for the injuries they inflict on their wives, nor should the law intervene. Provided he neither kills nor maims her, it is legal for a man to beat his wife when she wrongs him – for instance, when she is about to surrender her body to another man, when she contradicts or abuses him, or when she refuses, like a decent woman, to obey his reasonable commands. In all these and similar cases, it is the husband's office to be his wife's chastiser.

> PHILIPPE DE BEAUMANOIR 1246–96
> *Customs of the People of Beauvais*

A man beats his wife so badly that he has to call both the doctor and the apothecary, paying them twice.
Paying them twice?
Once for this time and once for the next!

> 17th-century German joke

If your wife gets an attack of nerves, the best medicine is a good thrashing.

> Provençal proverb

It is a well known fact that you can strike your wife's bottom if you wish, but you must not strike her face . . . I believe that reasonable chastisement should be the duty of every husband if his wife misbehaves.

SHERIFF GEORGE MACKAY
Kinghorn, Scotland 1975

Many women, whose faces were disfigured by blows from husbands far sweeter-tempered than her own, used to gossip together and complain of the behaviour of their men-folk. My mother would meet this complaint with another – about the women's tongues.

ST AUGUSTINE A.D. 354–430
Confessions

Whatever trials may be the lot of your married life, though they may magnify themselves to your crushed spirit as beyond the endurance of woman to bear, resolve to bear them; fall down upon your knees and pray to be enabled to bear them; pray for patience, pray for strength to resist the demon that would urge you to escape; bear unto death, rather than forfeit your fair name and your good conscience . . .

MRS HENRY WOOD 1814–87
East Lynne

Eaper Weaper, chimbley-sweeper,
Had a wife but couldn't keep her,
Had another, didn't love her,
Up the chimbley he did shove her.

Skipping song

There are many times, even in a normal marriage, when a man wishes he could get rid of his wife, but I have to send you to prison because you killed a woman at the prime of her life.

MR JUSTICE JUPP
Yorkshire 1981

A far less weighty motive roused the anger of Egnatius Metellus, who beat his wife to death because she had drunk some wine; and this murder, far from leading to his being denounced, was not even blamed. People considered that her exemplary punishment had properly expiated her offence against the laws of sobriety: for any woman who drinks wine immoderately closes her heart to every virtue and opens it to every vice.

VALERIUS MAXIMUS *c.* 10 B.C.–A.D. 50

There are only about 20 murders a year in London and many not at all serious – some are just husbands killing their wives.

COMMANDER G.H. HATHERILL
Scotland Yard 1954

Guilt of girl who said No

Between a woman's Yes and No
There is not room for a pin to go.

Old Spanish saying

The average number of times a woman says no to temptation is once, weakly.

Joke

Have you not heard it said full oft
A woman's nay doth stand for naught?

WILLIAM SHAKESPEARE 1564–1616
'The Passionate Pilgrim'

Women who say no do not always mean no. It is not just a question of saying no, it is a question of how she says it, how she shows and makes it clear. If she doesn't want it she only has to keep her legs shut and she would not get it without force and there would be marks of force being used.

JUDGE DAVID WILD
Cambridge 1982

GUILT OF GIRL WHO SAID NO

Pretty Alison Woodman is still haunted by guilt over her ex-fiancés rampage. Even though she ended their affair two years earlier, she blames herself for triggering his lust to kill . . .

First the 24-year-old psychopath bludgeoned his sister Linda and mother Margaret with a hammer.

Then, armed with three shotguns, he burst into the factory in Patchway, Bristol, where 21-year-old Alison worked.

But instead of shooting her he blasted two workmates to death, telling cowering Alison "This is your lucky day" . . .

Sun 1988

*H*erb at your feet

Drunken women make good mates for sadistic men because they often encourage men to be cruel to them physically and mentally.

ERIC BERNE
A Layman's Guide to Psychiatry and Psychoanalysis
1969

All forms of masochism are related, and in essence more or less female, from the wish to be eaten by the father in the cannibalistic oral phase, through that of being whipped or beaten by him in the sadistic-anal stage and of being castrated in the phallic stage, to the wish, in the adult feminine stage, to be pierced.

MARIE BONAPARTE
Female Sexuality 1953

What they love to yield
They would often rather have stolen. Rough seduction
Delights them, the boldness of near rape
Is a compliment.

OVID 43 B.C.–A.D. 17
The Art of Love

You know women as well as I do. They are only unwilling when you compel them, but after that they're as enthusiastic as you are.

> JEAN GIRAUDOUX 1882–1944
> *Tiger at the Gates*

Women are doormats and have been
The years these mats applaud.
They keep the men from going in
With muddy feet to God.

> MARY CAROLYN DAVIES

With many women I doubt whether there be any more effectual way of touching their hearts than ill-using them . . . If you wish to get the sweetest fragrance from the herb at your feet, tread on it and bruise it.

> ANTHONY TROLLOPE 1815–82
> *Miss Mackenzie*

What women want is not to be treated with respect and care. They want to be treated like shit. They seem to like it.

> JOHN STEED (M4 rapist/murderer) 1986

Woman is subjected through her own continuous necessary wish – a wish which is the condition of her morality – to be so subjected.

> JOHANN FICHTE 1762–1814
> *The Science of Rights*

Women resist in order to be conquered.

> Proverb

We're going to be a little bit feminine in this respect. Like a woman, we want to be attacked.

LORD CHARTERIS (provost of Eton) 1981

Virtuous women are seldom accosted by unwelcome sexual propositions or familiarities, obscene talk or profane language.

PHYLLIS SCHAFLY
Senate testimony 1981

There are nevertheless a few women who constantly find that men are exposing themselves to them. These repeated shocks, however, do not have the effect of deterring them from taking solitary walks on heaths and commons where exhibitionists are known to lurk; and the woman who complains that this experience often happens to her may generally be justly accused of seeking it out.

ANTHONY STORR
Sexual Deviation 1964

If you can't be with the one you love

'Tis sweet to think, that, where'er we rove,
We are sure to find something blissful and dear,
And that, when we're far from the lips we love,
We've but to make love to the lips we are near.

THOMAS MOORE 1779–1852
'The Time I've Lost'

If you can't be with the one you love,
Love the one you're with.

STEPHEN STILLS
Song 1970

A one-night stand ended in murder after a man stabbed a teenager 16 times to stop his girlfriend finding out that he had two-timed her, a court heard yesterday.

Pretty Amanda Hopkinson, 17, was left bleeding to death in a lovers' lane after she was knifed repeatedly. The court heard that 25-year-old wood machinist Kevin Downing had met Amanda one night last March and offered to drive her home.

They made love several times then it is alleged Downing stabbed her after attempting to strangle her . . .

Downing later confessed, said Mr Purnell, and allegedly said he had offered Amanda a lift, adding: "I thought my luck was in. I have my girlfriend but a change is as good as a rest."

Daily Express 1988

When I'm not near the girl I love, I love the girl I'm near.
Every femme that flutters by me is a flame that must be
  fanned.
When I can't fondle the hand I'm fond of,
I fondle the hand at hand.

E.Y. HARBURG & BURTON LANE
– from *Finian's Rainbow* 1947

> In this vain fleeting universe, a man
> Of wisdom has two courses: first, he can
> Direct his time to pray, to save his soul,
> And wallow in religious nectar-bowl;
> But, if he cannot, it is surely best
> To touch and hold a lovely woman's breast,
> And to caress her warm round hips, and thighs,
> And to possess that which between them lies.

BHARTHARI 5th/6th century

If I meet a single girl I want to take her off to bed. Some of them expect it. They walk around with a mattress on their backs in case they bump into anyone they like.

JIM DAVIDSON 1986

Women are sex objects whether they like it or not.

JUDGE ARCHIE SIMONSON
– in court at rape case, Wisconsin U.S.A. 1977

Emergency regulations, uniforms, drafting, service orders and a life of discipline cramp the freedom of many young men, and during the long periods of wartime training and waiting not a few of them got bored – 'browned off' was the common term. Some missed their wives or girlfriends and got into trouble with local girls and camp followers, or WAAFS or WRENS or ATS girls, urged on by long periods of sex starvation. So during the 'phony' and training periods of 1939–43 there was a steady flow of rapes (some with strangling or other violence), of assaults (some fatal) . . . all arising from the changes in life that were thrust by service conditions on ordinary people.

> PROFESSOR KEITH SIMPSON
> *Forty Years of Murder* 1978

gin and fuck it – n. a girl, usu. foreign au pair or tourist, who can allegedly be seduced for the price of a drink in certain pubs where such pick-ups congregate.

> JONATHON GREEN
> *The Dictionary of Contemporary Slang* 1984

People do not do these things deliberately . . . they do it as part of their culture.

> JOHN SCOTT-GARNER (president of the National
> Communication Union)
> – commenting on 'Give us a kiss' remarks and
> bottom pinching 1986

A man lying in the top bunk of a cross-channel steamer peered down at the girl in the bunk beneath and watched while the woman there removed her wig, false teeth and glass eye. Finally she unscrewed her artificial leg. When she realised the man was watching her she said angrily, "Well! What are you waiting for?"

"Miss", he replied, "you know damned well what I'm waiting for. Hurry up and unscrew it and throw it here!"

Joke

Women should be elusive, mysterious and chaste. And I think that every man's ideal – even though they pretend it isn't today – is to find the wonderful, charming, delightful girl who will surrender to them.

BARBARA CARTLAND 1974

Find 'em, feel 'em, fuck 'em, and forget 'em!

The Four F Club motto 1950s

Women enjoy'd (whate'er they've been)
Are like romances read, or sights once seen.

SIR JOHN SUCKLING 1609–42
'Against Fruition'

A man deeply in lust with his secretary took her to dinner, but had no luck, so he started buying her presents. But this too had little effect. Eventually he bought her a very expensive fur coat. She was overjoyed, and as she was trying it on the man said, "Your knickers are coming down."

The girl blushed, discreetly checked and replied, "Oh no they're not."

"Oh yes they are," said the man, "or that coat goes back to the shop."

Joke

Mr David Nathan, defending, said the man might have been forgiven for thinking he would end up in bed with the secretary. "The days of Sir Walter Raleigh are gone, and men don't carry strange ladies' washing and have coffee with them unless they think they are on to a good thing," he added.

News of the World 1982

Rape is a very difficult thing . . . a woman invites a chap home for coffee, takes off her coat, then her jacket and he fondles her and then they are on the bed and she says 'No, no, no' but he's wildly excited and got his pants down. Very difficult.

JUDGE CHRISTMAS HUMPHREYS 1976

Women do not realize all the implications of their coquetry.

LA ROCHEFOUCAULD 1613–80
Maxims

Impure

What are little girls made of?
Sugar and spice, and all that's nice,
That's what little girls are made of.

Nursery rhyme

We should look upon the female state as being as it were a deformity though one that occurs in the ordinary course of nature.

ARISTOTLE 384–322 B.C.
On the Soul

If her bowels and flesh were cut open, you would see what filth is covered by her white skin. If a fine crimson cloth covered a pile of foul dung, would anyone be foolish enough to love the dung because of it? . . . There is no plague which monks would dread more than woman: the soul's death.

ROGER DE CAEN d. 1095
Song of the Degradation of the World

Even seeing Tanha, Arati, and Raga (the daughters of Mara), there was not the least wish in me for sexual intercourse. What is this, thy daughter's body, but a thing full of water and excrement? I do not even want to touch it with my foot.

> BUDDHA
> – in conversation with Magandiya Magandiyasutta,
> *Atthakavagga* (Buddhist text)

Take her skin from her face and thou shalt see all loathesomeness under it . . . within she is full of phlegm, stinking, putrid excremental stuff.

ST JOHN CHRYSOSTOM ('Golden Mouth') *c.* A.D. 347–407

Woman . . . A dunghill covered with white and red.

> PHILIP STUBBES d. 1593
> *Anatomie of Abuses*

Woman is an all-devouring curse. In her body the evil cycle of life begins afresh, born out of lust engendered by blood and semen. Man emerges mixed with excrement and water, fouled with the impurities of woman. A wise man will avoid the contaminating society of women as he would the touch of bodies infested with vermin.

> *Mahābhārata* (Hindu text)

But if you are sick, or on a journey, or one of you come from the privy, or if ye have touched a woman, and ye cannot find water, then use a good surface of sand and wipe your faces and your hands therewith; verily God pardons and forgives.

> *Koran* (Islamic text)

Nothing so casts down the manly mind from its height as the fondling of a woman.

ST AUGUSTINE A.D. 354–430
Soliloquies

Q. Why are electric trains like women's breasts?
A. Because they were intended for children, but it's their fathers who play with them.

Joke

Do not desire women, those female demons, on whose breasts grow two lumps of flesh, who continually change their mind, who entice men, and then make a sport of them as slaves.

Kapila's Verses (Gaina text)

If you can see through a woman, you're wasting your time – all the best parts are on the outside.

Joke

The whole body of a woman is pudendal, even face and hand, without exception (absolutely).

'Hashiya on al Baydawi', *al Khafaji* (Islamic text)

Impure is that part of woman which is below the navel.

Satapatha Brāhmana (Hindu text)

Woman is a temple built over a sewer.

TERTULLIAN *c.* A.D. 160–225
On the Cult of Women

One evening at the club an architect and an engineer debated between themselves as to who created Woman.

"An architect," said the architect, "for she has such beautiful proportions, such artistic curves."

"No," said the engineer, "it must have been an engineer, for she is a masterpiece of practical engineering; a machine perfectly designed for reproduction."

As they could not agree, they took their case to an old judge for arbitration. The judge thought for a few minutes, and then gave his pronouncement.

"Woman was designed by neither an architect or an engineer. She was designed by a planner."

The architect and the engineer asked the judge to explain his answer.

"It's quite simple," said the judge. "Only a planner would have placed the pleasure palace between the water-works and the sewage disposal plant."

Joke

At present I tend to regard the feminine organ as something unclean or as a wound, not less attractive on that account, but dangerous in itself, like everything bloody, mucous, infected.

MICHEL LEIRIS
Age d'Homme 1946

hair pie – n. the vagina; fr. the pubic hair, plus pun on 'hare'; an example of sex = food, cf. finger pie

JONATHON GREEN
The Dictionary of Contemporary Slang 1984

A number of tradesmen one day did combine,
With a rum-ti-dum, tum-ti-tum terro,
To the best of their skill to make something divine,

With a row-de-dow, row-de-dow derro.

The first was a carpenter – he thought it fit,
With a rum-ti-dum, tum-ti-tum terro,
With a bonny broad axe to give it a slit,
With a row-de-dow, row-de-dow derro.

The next was a mercer so neat and so trim,
With a rum-ti-dum, tum-ti-tum terro,
And he with red satin did line it within,
With a row-de-dow, row-de-dow derro.

Then came a furrier, so bold and so stout,
With a rum-ti-dum, tum-ti-tum terro,
And he with a bearskin did fur it about,
With a row-de-dow, row-de-dow derro.

The fishmonger next and he was full bent,
With a rum-ti-dum, tum-ti-tum terro,
With ling and red herring to give it a scent,
With a row-de-dow, row-de-dow derro.

Then in came a parson so bold and so blunt,
With a rum-ti-dum, tum-ti-tum terro,
And to make it a Christian he called it a c___,
With a row-de-dow, row-de-dow derro.

> Song from *The Gentleman's Bottle Companion*
> 18th century

The word 'ling', as well as its normal meaning for a kind of sea fish, had a nineteenth-century slang meaning as the female sexual organ, as in the term 'ling-grappling'. It appears . . . that it was also applied to the female sexual odour. This definition is not recorded in Partridge's Dictionary of Slang and Unconventional English but he gives a twentieth-century Australian usage of the word as a 'stink'. It seems possible that there is an association of ideas here.

GEORGE SPEAIGHT
Bawdy Songs of the Early Music Hall 1975

How can this divine animal, full of reason and judgment, which we call man, be attracted by these obscene parts of woman, defiled with juices and located shamefully at the lowest part of the trunk?

DES LAURENS (French physician)

> Oh virtue, virtue! What art thou become,
> That man would leave thee for that toy, a woman,
> Made from the dross and refuse of a Man!

JOHN DRYDEN 1631–1700
The Spanish Fryar

> Whate'er was left unfit in the Creation
> To make a toad, after its ugly fashion,
> Of scraping from unfinished creatures had,
> Sure was the body of a woman made.
> Yet if there's some finer atoms daubed upon,
> Which makes her seem so beauteous to look upon.
> Nor better is a woman's end, nor can
> Born only to nightmare the soul of man.
> Nor is he only plagued by her birth.
> She is an universal curse unto the earth.
> Some say the ground with barrenness is curst
> Where in the morn she strains her body first.

MYSOGYNUS
A Satire on Women 1682

O violencies of women!
Why, they are creatures made up and compounded
Of all monsters, poisoned minerals
And sorcerous herbs that grow.

JOHN WEBSTER *c.* 1580–1625
The Devil's Law Case

Thus then should everyone consider well, and loathe and put away the form of woman.

Fo-Sho-Hing-Tsan-King (Buddhist text)

When she had sucked the marrow from my bones
And languorously I turned to her with a kiss,
Beside me suddenly I saw nothing more
Than a gluey-sided leather bag of pus!

CHARLES PIERRE BAUDELAIRE 1821–67

What are young women made of, made of?
What are young women made of?
Ribbons and laces
And sweet pretty faces,
That's what young women are made of.

Nursery rhyme

*I*nability *of having an orgasm*

Your women are your tilth; so come into your tillage how you choose; but do a previous good act for yourselves, and fear God, and know that ye are going to meet Him; and give good tidings unto those who do believe.

Koran (Islamic text)

The uterus has naturally an incredible desire to conceive and procreate. Thus it is anxious to have virile semen, desirous of taking it, drawing it in, sucking it, and retaining it.

JEAN L. LIEBAUT
'Thresor desremides secrets pour les maladies
des femmes' 1597

Erotic movements undesirable for wives:
Lascivious movements are of no use whatever to wives. For a woman forbids herself to conceive and fights against it, if in her delight she aids the man's action with her buttocks, making undulating movements with all her breast limp; for she turns the share clean away from the furrow and makes the seed fail of its place. Whores indulge in such motions for their own purposes, that they may not often conceive and lie pregnant, and at the same time that their intercourse

may be more pleasing to men; which our wives evidently have no need for.

LUCRETIUS *c*. 99–55 B.C.
On the Nature of Things

And just as a 'desire' arises from a conception of the brain, and this conception springs from some external object of desire, so also from the male, as being the more perfect animal, and, as it were, the most natural object of desire, does the natural (organic) conception arise in the uterus, even as the animal conception does in the brain.

WILLIAM HARVEY 1578–1657
On Conception

A man, feeling unwell, went to the doctor, who advised him to give up smoking, drinking and sex or he'd had it. After a little while the man returned to the doctor feeling miserable with no cigarettes. The doctor looked at him and relented – "Just one a day."

A few days later he was back at the doctors – he missed his booze. Understanding, the doctor said, "No spirits, mind, but you can have half a pint a day."

After a few more days he was back again. "All right," said the doctor, "have sex occasionally, but only with your wife – it's important that you have no excitement."

Joke

A well-bred woman does not seek carnal gratification, and she is usually apathetic to sexual pleasures. Her love is physical or spiritual, rather than carnal, and her passiveness in regard to coition often amounts to disgust for it; lust is seldom an element in a woman's character, and she is the preserver of chastity and morality. If women were as salacious as men, morality, chastity, and virtue would not exist and the world would be but one vast brothel.

DR O.A. WALL
Sex and Sex Worship 1932

If she is normally developed mentally, and well-bred, her sexual desire is small. If this were not so the whole world would become a brothel and marriage and family impossible.

J. KRAFFT-EBING 1840–1902
Psychopathia Sexualis

What I ask of a woman is to give her pleasure.

HENRI DE MONTHERLANT 1896–1972
Les Jeunes filles

Q. Ever see an ice-cube with a hole in it?
A. Yes, I was married to one for twenty years.

Joke

No passion in a woman can be lasting long.

SAMUEL PEPYS 1633–1703
Diary

A mortician who practised in Fife
Made love to the corpse of his wife.
'How could I know, Judge?
She was cold, and did not budge –
Just the same as she acted in life.'

Joke

Because emotions rule all sexual responses (including orgasm) a woman needs to review carefully her own personal attitudes about sex, her feelings about her husband and their relationship together. In some cases, the inability of having an orgasm is simply the unconscious refusal to have one, in order to get revenge on the husband.

DR DAVID REUBEN
Any Woman Can 1973

LOVELORN GUNMAN SPURNED BY BEAUTY KILLS HIS OWN FAMILY ... A man's fatal attraction for a woman who spurned his love may have led to one of America's worst cases of mass murder.

Police probing the case of a gunman who went on the rampage in a small town revealed last night that the massacre death toll had risen to sixteen.

Daily Express 1987

There seems little doubt that the man who has learned various mechanical ways to stimulate his sexual specificity in order to copulate with a women who he does not this moment desire is doing far more violence to his nature than the female who needs only to receive a male to whom she gives many other assents, but possibly not active desire.

MARGARET MEAD 1901–78
Male and Female

Within five days of being left by his girlfriend a man had committed rape, murder, robbery and arson and taken a family hostage, an Old Bailey jury was told yesterday.

Independent 1988

So also ought men to love their wives as their own bodies. He that loveth his wife loveth himself.

'St Paul to Timothy I', *Holy Bible* (Christian text)

The truth in question consists in the fact, undeniable to all those not rendered impervious to facts by preconceived dogma, that as I have put it elsewhere, while man has a sex, woman is a sex.

ERNEST BELFORD BAX (founder of the English Socialist
League) 1854–1926
The Fraud of Feminism

Looks

The perfect woman must be haughty, but not too beautiful
. . . she must be a slave to her clothes and her jewels.

SALVADOR DALI 1904–89

What else do they want in life but to be as attractive as
possible to men? Do not all their trimmings and cosmetics
have this end in view, and all their baths, fittings, creams,
scents, as well – and all those arts of making up, painting,
and fashioning the face, eyes and skin? Just so. And by
what other sponsor are they better recommended to men
than by folly?

DESIDERIUS ERASMUS c. 1467–1536
In Praise of Folly

A girl who was raped by 15 men has been accused of
shaming her town because she reported the attack.

The people of Mazzarino, Sicily, say 20-year-old Pina
Siracusa got what she deserved because she was "always
walking around the town in mini-skirts and smoking
cigarettes".

"She provoked the boys and they should never be
arrested for raping her – she deserved everything she got,"
said one citizen, Salvatore Malerba, whose view is shared
by most people in Mazzarino.

Daily Express 1988

Looks

Let no woman's painting breed thy stomach's fainting.

Proverb

Glamour is when a man knows a woman is a woman.

GINA LOLLOBRIGIDA 1956

Women are really all alike:
But, however, let her be one of the supremest dignity of countenance, let the power of Venus radiate from her whole body, the truth is there are others, the truth is we have lived so far without this one; the truth is she does all the same things as the ugly woman does, and we know it, fumigating herself, poor wretch, with rank odours while her maidservants give her a wide berth and giggle behind her back. But the lover shut out, weeping, often covers the threshold with flowers and wreaths, anoints the proud doorposts with oil of marjoram, presses his love-sick kisses upon the door; but if he is let in, once he gets but one whiff as he comes, he would seek some decent excuse for taking his leave; there would be an end of the complaint so often rehearsed, so deeply felt, and he would condemn himself on the spot of folly, now he sees that he has attributed to her more than it is right to concede to a mortal. Our Venuses are quite well aware of this; so they are at greater pains themselves to hide all that is behind the scenes of life from those they wish to detain fast bound in the chains of love.

LUCRETIUS *c.* 99–55 B.C.
On the Nature of Things

Turn away thy face from a woman dressed up: and gaze not about upon another's beauty. For many have perished by the beauty of a woman, and hereby lust is enkindled as a fire.

'Ecclesiasticus', *Holy Bible* (Judaeo-Christian text)

To the open view of all men they paint and embellish themselves with counterfeit and borrowed beauties. I have seen them swallow gravel, ashes, coals, dust, tallow candles and for the nonce labour and toil themselves to spoil their stomach only to get a pale bleak colour; to become slender in waist, and to have a narrow spagnolised body, what pinching, what girding, what cingling will they not endure; yea sometimes with iron plates, with whalebones and other such trash.

MICHEL DE MONTAIGNE 1533–92

My wife once put on a mudpack – it improved her appearance tremendously for a while. Then she took it off.

Joke

Men have often been taken in
By artless beauty. So when she's spreading all that
Mess on her face is another good time – do not be shy –
To visit and inspect her. You will find a thousand pots of
   make-up,
Colours and grease, that have melted and run
Down into her sweaty cleavage.

OVID 43 B.C.–A.D. 17
Cures for Love

Hair wax, rouge, honey, teeth you buy –
A multifarious store!
A mask at once would all supply,
Nor would it cost you more.

WILLIAM COWPER 1731–1800

Looks

A man is as old as he's feeling,
A woman as old as she looks.

MORTIMER COLLINS 1827–76
The Unknown Quantity

Most women are not as young as they're painted.

SIR MAX BEERBOHM 1872–1956
A Defence of Cosmetics

This, too, the Lord says: See what airs they put on, the women-folk of Sion, walk head in air, look about them with glancing eyes, click the trappings on their feet with mincing steps. Ay, but the Lord has his doom ready for them; bald of head and bare of temple the women of Sion shall know it. In one day the Lord will sweep away all their finery, the shoes with the rest; locket, and collar, necklace and bracelet and veil; hair-pin, ankle-ring, chain, scent-box, pendant, signet-ring and nose-ring; gala dress and gown and scarf, bodkin and mirror and shawl and riband and kerchief. There will be new fashions then; stench for scent, hempen rope for waist-band, baldness for curls, and hair shirt for stomacher.

'Isaiah', *Holy Bible* (Judaeo-Christian text)

Thou who wilt not love do this;
Learn of me what woman is.
Something made of thread and thrum;
A mere botch of ore and sun.
Pieces, patches, ropes of hair;
In-laid garbage everywhere.
Outside silk and outside lawn;
Scenes to cheat us neatly drawn.
False in legs and false in thighs,
False in breast, teeth, hair and eyes,

False in head and false enough;
Only true in shreds and stuff.

ROBERT HERRICK 1591–1674
'On women'

All women, of whatever age, rank, profession, or degree
who shall, after this Act, impose upon, seduce, and betray
into marriage any of His Majesty's subjects by virtue of
scents, paints, cosmetic washes, artificial teeth or false hair,
iron stays, bolstered hips, or high-heeled shoes, shall incur
the penalty of the law now in force against witchcraft and
like misdemeanours; and marriage under such circumstances, upon conviction of the offending parties, shall be
null and void.

Act of Parliament 1770

Prudery is a sort of make-up with which women enhance
their beauty.

LA ROCHEFOUCAULD 1613–80
Maxims

Oh the unsounded sea of women's bloods,
That when 'tis calmest, is most dangerous!
Not any wrinkle creaming in their faces,
When in their hearts are Scylla and Charybdis,
Which still are hid in dark and standing fogs,
Where never day shines, nothing ever grows,
But weeds and poisons that no statesman knows:
Not Cerberus ever saw the damned nooks,
Hid with the veils of women's virtuous looks.

GEORGE CHAPMAN *c.* 1559–1634
Bussy D'Ambois

Untaught to bear it, women talk away
To God himself, and fondly think they pray.

Women were made to give our eyes delight;
A female sloven is an odious sight.

EDWARD YOUNG 1683–1765
'On Women'

If a girl isn't pretty
Like the Miss Atlantic City,
All she gets from life is pity
And a pat.

BOB MERRILL
– from *Funny Girl* 1964

My only books
Were woman's looks
And folly's all they've taught me.

THOMAS MOORE 1779–1852
'This Life is all Chequered', *Irish Melodies*

Doth not even nature itself teach you that a man indeed, if he nourish his hair, it is a shame unto him? But, if a woman nourish her hair, it is a glory to her; for her hair is given to her for a covering.

'St Paul to the Ephesians', *Holy Bible* (Christian text)

A scissor-wielding maniac leapt out at a 13-year-old girl and cropped her hair in a bizarre attack. The terrified youngster was skating near her home in Connah's Quay, Clwyd, when the bearded man grabbed her.

As she tried to pull away he snipped off her locks just below the neck.

The girl managed to escape and raise the alarm.

But police hunting the stockily-built man warned: "He is very odd to say the least."

Sun 1988

Women have long hair and short brains.

Proverb

Even nature herself abhors to see a woman shorn or polled; a woman with cut hair is a filthy spectacle, and much like a monster; and all repute it a very great absurdity for a woman to walk abroad with shorn hair; for this is all one as if she should take upon her the form or person of a man, to whom short cut hair is proper, it being natural and comely to women to nourish their hair, which even God and nature have given them for a covering, a token of subjection, and a natural badge to distinguish them from men.

WILLIAM PRYNNE 1600–69
Histrio-Mastix

The two-year career of the Phantom Barber of Euston Station was cut short by Highbury Magistrates on Monday.

Fleet Street business analyst, Stephen Elms . . . would approach women with long hair from behind and snip away a lock on tube escalators while on his way to and from work. Thirty-three-year-old Elms pleaded guilty to four charges of common assault at Euston Station in 1986. He asked for 11 other similar offences to be taken into consideration.

Hemel Hempstead Herald 1988

Looks

There's nothing a woman
Baulks at, no action that gives her a twinge of conscience
Once she's put on her emerald choker, weighted down
　her ear-lobes
With vast pearl pendants. What's more insufferable
Than your well-heeled female?

JUVENAL *c.* A.D. 55–140
Satires

A policeman with a fetish for women's shoes was jailed for five years yesterday.

Charles Hay, 37, had terrorised among women for eight years, Edinburgh High Court heard. His victims ranged from a 16-year-old girl to a 66-year-old woman.

He once visited a 22-year-old whose husband was in prison. He attacked her, tied tights round her neck, forced her to remove her underwear and to put on a pair of boots. He then bit and licked the boots.

Charles Hay, with 18 years service and awards for bravery, admitted 13 offences in Musselburgh, Leith and Joppa, suburbs of Edinburgh.

Mr. George Penrose, QC, prosecuting, said Hay once pretended he was a representative and got a woman to try on shoes he brought to her house. He held a knife to her throat, then kissed her. He also attacked a 16-year-old girl who was carrying a kitten. He pulled her to the ground and ran off with her shoes.

Hay was finally caught after he robbed a woman of her shoes and a police sergeant recognised him from details she gave the police.

Mr. Hugh Campbell, QC for Hay, said it had gone beyond a simple shoe fetish and he needed treatment.

Hay, formerly of Dalrymple Loan, Musselburgh, who is married with two children, has resigned from the police.

Liverpool Post 1986

Males are more active in seeking sexual stimuli in the environment, and if, as a result of early learning, adolescent knockbacks, or inferiority feelings arising from any source, women become classified as unapproachable, they will turn to near approximations of women, e.g. children, underwear, sheep, rubber blow-ups . . .

DR GLENN WILSON
British Journal of Sexual Medicine 1981

Low sloppy beasts

Let me get my hands on your mammary glands,
Let me get your head on the conjugal bed
I say, I say, I say I crack the whip
And you skip but you deserve it.

MORRISSEY (of The Smiths)
'Handsome Devil' 1984

Most men who understand women at all feel hostility toward them. At their worst, women are low sloppy beasts.

NORMAN MAILER
The Presidential Papers 1963

Run and hide in osiers, twot,
Cause here you suitors come!
Hirsute Hank, Testicle Tom
and Indrick the Dick himself.

Daddy grinds and grinds mommy
As if he wants to grind her down.
He rests a little in-between
Then he starts to grind again.

Canter, blackie, tra-la-la,
Tomorrow we hit Riga.
We'll kidnap young broads
And drill into old hags.

Gramps goes to tend cattle
He puts a chisel in his bag
When he encounters a black spot
He'll chisel a hole in it.

Latvian folksong

I hate women because they always know where things are.

JAMES THURBER 1894–1961

Let everyone loathe his lady and be ashamed to be her servant . . . fly women.

JOHN LYLY c. 1554–1606
Euphues

I . . . hate women because they almost never get anything exactly right.

JAMES THURBER 1894–1961
'The Case Against Women'

"I hate women," he thought savagely. "They're bold, brazen, abominable creatures, invented for the annoyance and destruction of their superiors."

MARY ELIZABETH BRADDON 1837–1915
Lady Audley's Secret

I'm not a woman hater. Life is only long enough to allow even an energetic man to hate one woman – adequately.

FRANK RICHARDSON
Mayfair no. 2835

No war without a woman.

Proverb

For Pandora brought in her arms a great vase – which is incorrectly called 'Pandora's Box'. She raised its lid and the terrible afflictions with which the vase had been filled escaped and spread over the earth. Hope alone did not fly away. Thus, with the arrival of the first woman, misery made its appearance on earth.

'Greek mythology', *New Larousse Encyclopaedia of Mythology* 1968

MOTHERS WHO WORK BLAMED FOR
CHILD CRIME
The Chief Constable of Bedfordshire was yesterday criticised for blaming working mothers for the rise in juvenile crime and telling them to stay at home.

Daily Telegraph 1988

From the woman came the beginning of sin, and by her we all die.

'Ecclesiasticus', *Holy Bible* (Judaeo-Christian text)

Man may escape from rope and gun;
Nay, some have outliv'd the doctor's pill:
Who takes a woman must be undone,
That basilisk is sure to kill.
The fly that sips treacle is lost in the sweets,
So he that tastes woman, woman, woman,
He that tastes woman, ruin meets.

JOHN GAY 1685–1732
The Beggar's Opera

But the leader of all wickedness is woman; 'tis she, cunning mistress of crime, besets our minds; 'tis by her foul adulteries so many cities smoke, so many nations war, so many peoples lie crushed beneath the ruins of their kingdoms, utterly o'erthrown. Let others be unnamed; Aegeus' wife alone, Medea, will prove that women are an accursed race . . . I abominate them all, I dread, shun, curse them all. Be it reason, be it instinct, be it wild rage: 'tis my joy to hate them. Sooner shall you mate fire and water, sooner shall the dangerous Syrtes offer to ships a friendly passage, sooner shall Tethys from her far western shore bring in bright dawn, and wolves gaze on does with eyes caressing, than I, my hate o'ercome, have kindly thought for woman.

SENECA *c.* 58 B.C.–A.D. 65
Hippolytus

The female sex wholly govern domestic life: and by this means, when they think fit, they can sow dissensions between the dearest friends, may make father and son irreconcilable enemies, in spite of all the ties of gratitude on one part, and the duty of protection to be paid on the other.

SIR RICHARD STEELE 1672–1729
Spectator

If you don't want trouble, don't go near a woman.

PETER O'TOOLE 1988

The sadness of the heart is every plague: and the wickedness of a woman is all evil. And a man will choose any plague, but the plague of the heart: And any wickedness but the wickedness of a woman . . . There is no head worse than the head of a serpent: And there is no anger above the anger of a woman. It will be more agreeable to abide with a lion and a dragon, than to dwell with a wicked woman.

'Ecclesiasticus', *Holy Bible* (Judaeo-Christian text)

Low sloppy beasts

A clever man will build a city, a clever woman will lay it low.

Chinese proverb

Nearly all the kingdoms of the world have been overthrown by women.

JACOB SPRENGER & HENDRICH KRAMER
Malleus Maleficarum (the indispensable handbook and
ultimate authority for the Inquisition) 1489

But no marvel it is for a fool to act madly
Through woman's wiles to be brought to woe.
So for certain was Adam deceived by some woman.
By several Solomon, Samson besides;
Delilah dealt him his doom and David
Was duped by Bath-Sheba, enduring much sorrow.
Since these were grieved by their guile twould be great
    gain
To love them yet never believe them, if knights could.

Sir Gawain and the Green Knight 14th century

Well, a hard headed woman, a soft hearted man
Been the cause of trouble ever since the world began.
Oh yeah, ever since the world began.
A hard headed woman been a thorn in the side of man.

Adam told Eve: listen here to me;
Don't you let me catch you messin' round that apple tree.

Now Samson told Delilah loud and clear,
Keep your cotton pickin' fingers out my curly hair.

I heard 'bout a king who was doing swell
Till he started playing with that evil Jezebel.

Well, a hard headed woman, a soft hearted man

Been the cause of trouble ever since the world began.
Oh yeah, ever since the world began.
A hard headed woman been a thorn in the side of man.

CLAUDE DE METRIUS
– sung by Elvis Presley in *King Creole* 1958

The eastern potentate who declared that women were at the bottom of all mischief should have gone a little further and seen why it is so. It is because women are *never lazy*. They don't know what it is to be quiet. They are Semiramides, and Cleopatras, and Joan of Arcs, Queen Elizabeths, and Catherine the Seconds, and they riot in battle, and murder, and clamour, and desperation. If they can't agitate the universe and play at ball with hemispheres, they'll make mountains out of warfare and vexation out of domestic mole-hills; and social storms in household teacups. Forbid them to hold forth upon the freedom of nations and the wrongs of mankind, and they'll quarrel with Mrs. Jones about the shape of a mantle or the character of a small maid-servant. To call them the weaker sex is to utter a hideous mockery. They are the stronger sex, the noisier, the more persevering, the most self-assertive sex. They want freedom of opinion, variety of occupation, do they? Let them have it. Let them be lawyers, doctors, preachers, teachers, soldiers, legislators – anything they like – but let them be quiet – if they can.

MARY ELIZABETH BRADDON 1837–1915
Lady Audley's Secret

A woman sows the seed of quarrel.

'Prakriti-Khanda', *Brahma-Vaivarta* (Hindu text)

Of all the evil, the worst evil I have ever seen is the female sex: the hindrance, the hatred, the low calculation, the crudity, above all the inhuman threat to a spirit that wants to grow, to rise.

AUGUST STRINDBERG 1849–1912

A woman who meditates alone meditates evil.

PUBLIUS SYRUS 1st century B.C.
Opinions

Evil comes from the darkness of women.

ANTONIN ARTAUD (French playwright) 1896–1948

All women are evil and are to blame for all the evil in the world.

SHIRLEY BASSEY 1967

If we but seriously consider the nature and qualities of the generality of the sex, even in all ages from the fall of man to this present, we may well perceive that they have not only been extremely evil in themselves, but have also been the main instruments and immediate causes of murder, idolatry, and a multitude of other heinous sins, in many high and eminent men.

A Briefe Anatomie of Women 1653

The former wife of the man accused of the Railway Murders told an Old Bailey jury today of their stormy marriage and said he once boasted of raping a girl. Mrs. Margaret Duffy said that her ex-husband John told her that the attack was her fault.

Evening Standard 1988

Woman, the fountain of all human frailty!
What mighty ills have not been done by woman?
Who was't betrayed the Capitol? A woman.
Who lost Mark Anthony the world? A woman.
Who was the cause of a long ten years' war,
And laid at last Old Troy in ashes? A woman.
Destructive, damnable, deceitful woman.
Woman, to man first as a blessing giv'n
When innocence and love were in their prime!
Happy a while in Paradise they lay;
But quickly woman longed to go astray;
Some foolish new adventure needs must prove
And the first devil she saw she changed her love;
To his temptations lewdly she inclined
Her soul, and for an apple damned mankind.

THOMAS OTWAY 1652–85
The Orphan

Possibly never in the history of Europe has the influence of women been so marked, both openly and sub rosa, in political life as during the past ten years.

Few realise that much of the suffering now being endured is due to that influence.

There are not many women who can resist the temptation to participate in some form of political intrigue. It gives them a false sense of power and domination, and appeals to their natures. Even the torrents of abuse and often gross slander heaped upon them only serves to flatter their vanity . . .

Long ago Adolf Hitler, keen student of psychology and astute politician, realised that women in all countries could be used to further his aims . . . The hidden hand of Hitler has guided and controlled. Women have worked on his behalf often in complete ignorance that they were being used as the instruments which would assist in the downfall of their own country.

RICHARD BAXTER
Guilty Woman 1941

HITLER WAS A WOMAN

Front page headline, *Sunday Sport* 1988

Do not let her steal thy heart away, do not be enticed by her beckoning. Many the wounds such a woman has dealt; a brave retinue she has of men murdered; truly her house is the grave's ante-chamber, opens the door into the secret closet of death.

'Proverbs', *Holy Bible* (Judaeo-Christian text)

Of all the plagues with which the world is curst,
Of every ill, a woman is the worst.

GEORGE GRANVILLE 1667–1735
The British Enchanters

These then are the twenty-two troubles declared by the venerable Ascetic Mahavira which a monk must learn and know, bear and conquer, in order not to be vanquished by them when he lives the life of a wandering mendicant.

1 hunger
2 thirst
3 cold
4 heat
5 gad-flies and gnats
6 nakedness
7 to be discontented with the objects of control
8 women
9 erratic life

10 place for study
11 lodging
12 abuse
13 corporal punishment
14 to ask for something
15 to be refused
16 illness
17 pricking of grass
18 dirt
19 kind and respectful treatment
20 understanding
21 ignorance
22 righteousness

Uttarâdhyayana (Gaina text)

Many young men drift along with the rest of the crowd according to chance and thus never reach happiness. From being passive be active. Don't drift. Take your own line. Paddle your own canoe. Only mind the rocks! Avoid them by cultivating other qualities.

The Rocks: 1 Horses
            2 Wine
            3 Women
            4 Cuckoos
            5 Irreligion

SIR ROBERT BADEN-POWELL 1857–1941
Rovering to Success

No mischief but a woman or a priest is at the bottom of it.

Proverb

If, Ananda, women had not received permission to go out from the household life and enter the homeless state under the doctrine and discipline proclaimed by the Tathagata, then would the pure religion, Ananda, have lasted long, the good law would have stood fast for a thousand years. But since, Ananda, women have now received that permission, the pure religion, Ananda, will not now last so long; the good law will now stand fast for only 500 years. Just, Ananda, as houses in which there are many women and but few men are easily violated by robber burglars; just so, Ananda, under whatever doctrine and discipline women are allowed to go out from the household life into the homeless state, that religion will not last long. And just, Ananda, as when the disease called mildew falls upon a field of rice in fine condition, that field of rice does not continue long; just so, Ananda, under whatever doctrine and discipline women are allowed to go out from the household life into the homeless state, that religion will not last long. And just, Ananda, as when the disease called blight falls upon a field of sugar cane in good condition, that field of sugar cane does not continue long; just so, Ananda, under whatever doctrine and discipline women are allowed to go out from the household life into the homeless state, that religion will not last long.

Kullavagga (Buddhist text)

Tarry not among women. For from garments cometh a moth; and from a woman the iniquity of man. For better is the iniquity of a man, than a woman doing a good turn and a woman bringing shame and reproach.

'St Paul to the Corinthians I', *Holy Bible* (Christian text)

> Lor' but women's rum cattle to deal with!
> The first found that to his cost,
> And I reckon it's just through a woman
> The last man on earth'll be lost.

GEORGE ROBERT SIMS 1847–1922
'Moll Jarvis O'Morley'

Make him a slave

You're as charming as you're tractable,
Every grace to tease the eye.
Since the angels lend their ways to you,
You can please us when you try,
You can please us when you try.
But you girls you're always, always, always at it,
Always at it for I cannot tell a lie,
No, I cannot tell a lie.
I have found the sex congenial, merely venial.
You intention's always splendid,
I've defended every grace to tease the eye,
When you try.
Girls, girls, girls, why are you always at it,
Yes, always, always at it,
Yes, always at it, at it, at it, at it.
When the men say girls be dratted,
Well we know the reason why,
The reason why . . . [to be continued]

LORENZO DA PONTE 1749–1838
– from Mozart's *Cosi fan Tutte*

Females are naturally libidinous, incite the males to copulation, and cry out during the act of coition.

ARISTOTLE 384–22 B.C.
Historia Animalium

Make him a slave

The instinct to flirt is fundamental to the feminine temperament, but not all women give it free rein because in some it is held in check by fear or common sense.

LA ROCHEFOUCAULD 1613–80
Maxims

It is the nature of women to seduce men. For that reason the wise are never unguarded in women's company. For women can lead astray not only a fool, but even a learned man, and make him a slave of desire and anger. One should not sit in a lonely place with one's mother, sister, or daughter; for the senses are powerful and master even a learned man.

Laws of Manu (Hindu text)

Though you seek here, there, everywhere,
Every woman is a whore.

JEAN DE MEUN *c.* 1240–1305
Roman de la Rose

Sexual compulsion
Drives women to worse crimes: lust is their strongest
motive.

JUVENAL *c.* A.D. 55–140
Satires

'Tis woman that seduces all mankind.

JOHN GAY 1685–1732
The Beggar's Opera

Now all my kind by me is kente
To flee women's enticement;

Who trusteth them in any intent,
Truly he is deceived.
My lecherous wife hath been my foe,
The devil's envy hath shent me also:
These two together well may go,
The sister and the brother.

'The Creation and Fall', Chester Mystery Cycle,
14th century

'How are we to conduct ourselves, Lord, with regard to
womankind?'
   'Don't see them, Ananda.'
   'But if we should see them, what are we to do?'
   'Abstain from speech, Ananda.'
   'But if they should speak to us, Lord, what are we to do?'
   'Keep wide awake, Ananda.'

Maha-Parinibbâna-Sutta (Buddhist text)

My destiny has been cast among cocksure women. Perhaps
when man begins to doubt himself, women, who should be
nice and peacefully hen-sure, become instead inostensibly
cocksure. She develops convictions, and she catches men.
And then woe betide everybody.

D.H. LAWRENCE 1885–1930
Phoenus: Art and Morality

Ashes to ashes,
Dust to dust.
If whiskey don't get you,
Women must.

Book of Negro Humour ed. Langston Hughes

Women are evil temptresses.

al Bukhari (Islamic text)

First, give no credence to the wiles of woman; honey-sweet words the temptress may use, all her talk be soothing as oil, but oh, the dregs of that cup are bitter; a two-edged sword brings no sharper pang. Death's road she follows, her feet set towards the grave; far from the highway that leads to life is the maze she treads. Heed, then, my warning, and depart from it never; shun her company, do not go near her doors. Wouldst thou squander the pride of thy manhood upon heartless strangers like these?

'Proverbs', *Holy Bible* (Judaeo-Christian text)

Away, away – you're all the same,
A fluttering, smiling, jilting throng!

THOMAS MOORE 1779–1852
'Woman'

The whole world is strewn with snares, traps, gins and pitfalls for the capture of men by women.

GEORGE BERNARD SHAW 1856–1950
Man and Superman

No fowler lays abroad more nets for his game or hunter for his prey than you to catch poor innocent man.

GEORGE FARQUHAR *c.* 1677–1707
The Inconstant

Give not the power of thy soul to a woman: lest she enter upon thy strength, and thou be confounded.

'Ecclesiastes', *Holy Bible* (Judaeo-Christian text)

For women, with a mischief to their kind,
Pervert with bad advice our better mind;
A woman's counsel brought us first to woe,
And made her man his paradise forgo.

JOHN DRYDEN 1631–1700
'The Cock and the Fox'

Of women's unnatural, insatiable lust, what country, what village doth not complain.

ROBERT BURTON 1577–1640
Anatomy of Melancholy

Better fall into the fierce tiger's mouth or under the sharp knife of the executioner, than to dwell with a woman and excite in yourselves lustful thoughts. A woman is anxious to exhibit her form and shape, whether walking, standing, sitting or sleeping. Even when represented as a picture she desires most of all to set off the blandishments of her beauty, and thus to rob men of their steadfast heart! How then ought you to guard yourselves? By regarding her tears and her smiles as enemies, her stooping form, her hanging arms, and all her disentangled hair as toils designed to entrap man's heart. Then how much more should you suspect her studied, amorous beauty! When she displays her dainty outline, her richly ornamented form, and chatters gaily with the foolish man! Ah then! What perturbation and what evil thoughts not seeing underneath the horrid tainted shape, the sorrows or impermanence, the impurity, the unreality! Considering these as the reality, all lustful thoughts die out.

Fo-Sho-Hing-Tsan-King (Buddhist text)

Make him a slave

Most women have small waists the world throughout,
But their desires are a thousand miles about.

CYRIL TOURNEUR *c.* 1575–1626
The Revenger's Tragedy

An unusually sexually promiscuous young lady.

JUDGE WILLIAM REINECKE
– on a girl, aged five, who had been sexually assaulted
by her mother's boyfriend, Wisconsin USA 1982

[continued]
    Darling girls you're always at it.
    When the men say girls be dratted,
    Well we know the reason why,
    The reason why! But why,
    But why do we know the reason why?
    But why, but why do we know the reason why,
    The reason why, the reason why,
    Do we know the reason why?

LORENZO DA PONTE 1749–1838
– from Mozart's *Cosi fan Tutte*

Mind of a woman

Women are irrational,
That's all there is to that.
Their heads are full of cotton, hay and rags.
They're nothing but exasperating, irritating, vacillating,
   calculating, agitating, maddening and infuriating hags.
Pickering, why can't a woman be more like a man . . .
Why is thinking something women never do, why is logic
   never even tried?
Straightening out their hair is all they ever do,
Why don't they straighten the mess that's inside?

ALAN JAY LERNER
'A Hymn to Him', *My Fair Lady* 1956

Extraordinarily important parts of the brain necessary for
spiritual life, the frontal convolutions and the temporal
lobes, are less well developed in women and this difference
is inborn.

P. MOEBIUS
'The physiological intellectual feebleness of women' 1907

But, no matter. Merlin told me once never to be too
disturbed if you don't understand what a woman is thinking – they don't do it often.

ALAN JAY LERNER
'How to Handle a Woman', *Camelot* 1960

'When she beat me on the verbal stakes, I could always beat her on the physical.'

PHIL (wife-beater)
Men on Violence ITV 1988

The majority of the dwellers of Hell will be women who curse too much and are ungrateful to their spouses – The Messenger of Allah observed: 'O, Womenfolk, you should give charity and ask much forgiveness for I saw you in bulk amongst the dwellers of Hell.' A wise lady among them said: 'Why is it, Messenger of Allah, that our folk is in bulk in the Hell?' Upon this the Holy Prophet observed: 'You curse too much and are ungrateful to your spouses. Also you lack common-sense . . . and rob wisdom of the wise.' Upon this the woman remarked: 'What is wrong with our common-sense . . . ?' The Holy Prophet observed: 'Your lack of common-sense can well be judged from the fact that the evidence of two women is equal to one man – that is a proof of the lack of common-sense.'

'Sahih', *Muslim ibn Hajjaj* (Islamic text)

The weakness of their reasoning faculty also explains why women show more sympathy for the unfortunate than men . . . and why on the contrary they are inferior to men as regards justice, and less honourable and conscientious.

ARTUR SCHOPENHAUER 1788–1860
On Women

The mind of woman brooks not discipline. Her intellect hath little weight.

Rig Veda (Hindu text)

Most women are bird-brained . . . It's rare to find a woman with very good mental agility.

> EARL SPENCER (father of the Princess of Wales) 1987

Intellectually, a certain inferiority of the female sex can hardly be denied . . . Women are intellectually more desultory and volatile than men; they are more occupied with particular instances than with general principles; they judge rather by intuitive perceptions than by deliberate reasoning.

> W.E.H. LECKY 1838–1903
> *History of European Morals II*

A very little wit is valued in a woman, as we are pleased with a few words spoken plain by a parrot.

> JONATHAN SWIFT 1667–1745
> *Thoughts on Various Subjects*

Having been asked to answer the question 'Are witty women attractive to men', I answer decidedly 'No'.

> STEPHEN LEACOCK 1869–1944
> 'Are witty women attractive to men?'

A woman with a beard is not so disgusting as a woman who acts the freethinker.

> JOHN CASPAR LAVATER (1741–1801)
> *Essays on Physionomy*

If girls aren't ignorant, they're cultured . . . You can't avoid suffering.

> WILLIAM COOPER
> *Scenes from Provincial Life* 1950

Monsters of creation

Learned ladies are not to my taste.

MOLIÈRE 1622–73
Les Femmes savantes

ANTRONIUS: It isn't feminine to be intellectual; women are made for pleasure . . .

MAGDALA: Is it not a woman's business to mind the affairs of her family and to instruct her children?

ANTRONIUS: Yes, it is.

MAGDALA: And do you think so weighty an office can be performed without wisdom?

ANTRONIUS: I believe not.

MAGDALA: This wisdom I can learn from books . . .

ANTRONIUS: I can tolerate books – but not Latin ones.

MAGDALA: Why so?

ANTRONIUS: Because that tongue is not fit for a woman.

MAGDALA: I want to know the reason.

ANTRONIUS: Because it contributes nothing towards the defence of their chastity . . . The common people think as I do, because it is such a rare and unusual thing for a woman to understand Latin . . .

MAGDALA: Why then is it not becoming for me to learn Latin, that I may be able daily to have conversation with so many eloquent, learned and wise authors and faithful counsellors?

ANTRONIUS: Books destroy women's brains who have little
enough of them . . . Bookishness makes folk mad . . . By
my faith, I would not have a learned wife . . . I have often
heard it said that a wise woman is twice a fool . . .

DESIDERIUS ERASMUS 1466–1536
Colloquies

A man who teaches women letters feeds more poison to
a frightful asp.

MENANDER *c.* 343–291 B.C.
Fragments

Women acquire learning – we know not how – almost as if
by breathing ideas, more by living really than by actually
taking hold of knowledge. Man, on the other hand,
achieves his distinction only by means of advancing
thought and much skilled exertion.

GEORG HEGEL 1770–1831
The Philosophy of Right

A learned girl is one of the most intolerable monsters of
creation.

Saturday Review 1870

We will strangle higher education for women.

DR WAGNER (Nazi Medical Officer) 1934

On the face of it the formal school and university structure
today made the curious assumption that men and women
were socially interchangeable, he said. They were taught
the same things and made to compete in the same examin-
ations leading to the same degrees without any regard for

the fact that as soon as they went out into the adult world they would be expected to lead entirely different lives.

By experience women were being taught to be contemptuous of their own femininity, so society now found itself extremely short of people willing to undertake the basic jobs previously assumed to be the only allocation of women.

Dr Leach said women still had to look after the children, do the cooking, and manage the domestic chores, but they did the jobs without goodwill.

Instead of training our women to be imitation second class males we should recognize the basic facts of existence and make a clear distinction between male and female roles, concentrating our attention on raising the social status of the female role, he said.

> *The Times* reporting speech of Dr Edmund Leach, provost of King's College, Cambridge to the British Humanist Association Conference 1969

If you have a female child, set her to sewing and not to reading, for it is not suitable for a female to know how to read unless she is going to be a nun ... teach her to do everything about the house, to make bread, clean capons, sift, cook, launder, make beds, spin, weave French purses, embroider, cut wool and linen clothes, put new feet on to socks, and so forth, so that when you marry her off she won't seem a fool freshly arrived from the wilds.

> PAOLO DA CERTALDO *c.* 1300–70
> *Libro di buoni costumi*

A man is in general better pleased when he has a good dinner upon his table than when his wife talks Greek.

> SAMUEL JOHNSON 1709–84

But – Oh! ye lords of ladies intellectual,
Inform us truly, have they not hen-peck'd you all?

GEORGE, LORD BYRON 1788–1824
Don Juan

Many women write with charm, style, wit, sympathy,
sensitivity, grace – but they do not write with greatness.

WAVERLEY ROOT
'Women are intellectually inferior' 1949

Mrs [Elizabeth Barrett] Browning's death is rather a relief
to me, I must say. No more Aurora Leighs, thank God! A
woman of real genius, I know; but what is the upshot of it
all? She and her sex had better mind the kitchen and the
children; and perhaps the poor. Except in such things as
little novels, they only devote themselves to what men do
much better, leaving that which men do worse or not at
all.

EDWARD FITZGERALD 1809–93
Life & Letters

Literature cannot be the business of a woman's life, and it
ought not to be. The more she is engaged in her proper
duties, the less leisure will she have for it, even as an
accomplishment and a recreation. To those duties you have
not yet been called, and when you are you will be less eager
for celebrity. You will not seek in imagination for excitement, of which the vicissitudes of this life, and the anxieties
from which you must not hope to be exempted, be your
state what it may, will bring with them but too much.

ROBERT SOUTHEY 1774–1843
Letter to Charlotte Brontë

I hate a learned woman.

EURIPIDES *c.* 480–406 B.C.
Hippolytus

When a woman inclines to learning, there is usually something wrong with her sex apparatus.

F.W. NIETZSCHE 1844–1900

In regard to the possible effect on health and physical vigour of women students, it was feared that the opening of new facilities for study and intellectual improvement would result in the creation of a new race of puny, sedentary and unfeminine students, and would destroy the grace and charm of social life, and would disqualify women for their true vocation, the nurture of the coming race and the governance of well-ordered, healthy and happy homes.

J. FITCH
'Women in the Universities', *Contemporary Review* 1890

Girls should be educated in terms of their own social function – which is to make for themselves, their children and their husbands a secure and suitable home, and to be mothers.

SIR JOHN NEWSOM (Chairman of British Government advisory panel on women's education) 1963

The aim of feminine education is invariably to be the future mother.

ADOLF HITLER 1889–1945
Mein Kampf

We like the lady who rides, rows or rinks,
But not the lady who makes pious fuss,
Or the she-philosopher who thinks she thinks
And studies Sanskrit or the calculus,
Or hunts midst polypi for missing links.
When these appear we ask why this is thus.

Punch 1876

'They hunt old trails' said Cyril 'very well;
But when did woman ever yet invent?'

ALFRED, LORD TENNYSON 1809–92
The Princess

Science seldom renders men amiable; women never.

EDMONE-PIERRE CHANVOT DE BEAUCHÊNE
1748–1824

Maurice, a beginner in X-ray diffraction work, wanted
some professional help and hoped that Rosy, a trained
crystallographer, could speed up his research. Rosy, however, did not see the situation this way . . . I suspect that in
the beginning Maurice hoped that Rosy would calm down.
Yet mere inspection suggested that she would not easily
bend. By choice she did not emphasise her feminine qualities. Though her features were strong, she was not
unattractive and might have been quite stunning had she
taken even a mild interest in clothes. This she did not.
There was never lipstick to contrast with her straight black
hair, while at the age of thirty-one her dresses showed all
the imagination of English blue-stocking adolescents. So
it was quite easy to imagine her the product of an unsatisfied mother who unduly stressed the desirability of
professional careers that could save bright girls from

marriages to dull men . . . Clearly Rosy had to go or be put in her place.

JAMES D. WATSON
– on Rosalind Franklin, whose X-ray analysis work and research into nuclear proteins made possible the correct analysis of DNA, *The Double Helix* 1968

Men seldom make passes at a girl who surpasses.

FRANKLIN P. JONES

I just don't like women telling jokes or making a spectacle of themselves. I can't think of one woman comic who makes me laugh.

JIM DAVIDSON 1986

A female poet, a female author of any kind, ranks below an actress, I think.

CHARLES LAMB 1775–1834

Man creates, woman conserves, man composes, woman interprets, man generalises, woman particularises . . . man thinks more than he feels, woman feels more than she thinks.

EARL BARNES 1861–1935
Woman in Modern Society

There are no women composers, never have been, and possibly never will be.

SIR THOMAS BEECHAM 1879–1961

The tongue of a woman is capable of producing sound, which admits of no comparison either for frightfulness or harmony.

Characters and Observations early 18th century

Singers in the church have a real liturgical office, and, therefore, women, as being incapable of exercising such office, cannot be admitted to form part of the choir or of the musical chapel.

POPE PIUS X 1835–1914

There's no music when a woman is in the concert.

THOMAS DEKKER *c.* 1570–1641
The Honest Whore

Consort not with a female musician lest thou be taken in by her snares.

BEN SIRA *c.* 190 B.C.
The Book of Wisdom

Nature never intended the fair sex to become cornetists, trombonists, and players of wind instruments . . . Women cannot possibly play brass instruments and look pretty, and why should they spoil their good looks?

GUSTAVE KERKER (musical director at the Casino Theatre, New York) 1930

The sight of girls . . . handling their double bass and blowing into the bassoon did not much please me.

MRS HESTER THRALE 1741–1821
Observations and Reflections

Women ruin music. If the ladies are ill-favoured the men do not want to play next to them, and if they are well-favoured they can't.

SIR THOMAS BEECHAM 1879–1961

Imagine with yourself what an unsightly matter it were to see a woman play upon a tabor or drum, or blow in a flute or trumpet or any like instrument: and this is because the boisterousness of them doth both cover and take away that sweet mildness which setteth so forth every deed that a woman doth.

BALDASSARE CASTIGLIONE 1478–1529
Book of the Courtier

To hear Bach, for instance, with 'feminine charm' smeared all over him by some of our young lady pianists is an indescribably nauseating experience. Moreover, women performers are quite shameless and unscrupulous in the way in which they so constantly trail the sexual red-herring across the path of the public's better judgement. The smirks, the mops and mows, the frank appeal to the basely sentimental side of the public's nature, which can never resist the 'charming girl' business, are simply so many devices to distract attention from musical shortcomings.

KAIKHOSRU SORABJI
Around Music 1932

The serious intrusion of women into Art would be an irremediable disaster.

GUSTAV MOREAU 1826–98

No woman can paint.

JOHN RUSKIN 1819–1900

Howe'er man rules in science and in art,
The sphere of woman's glories is the heart.

THOMAS MOORE 1779–1852
Epilogue to *Ina*

Women should not be expected to write, or fight, or build,
or compose scores; she does all by inspiring man to do all.

RALPH WALDO EMERSON 1803–82
Journals

Only the untalented woman is virtuous.

CONFUCIUS 551–479 B.C.

Nature has determined a woman's destiny

I am very fond of ladies. I like their beauty, I like their delicacy, I like their vivacity, and I like their silence.

SAMUEL JOHNSON 1709–84

[Women are] little balls of fluff in the eyes of the Creator. It's an endearing term I would use to describe my wife.

DONALD POMERLEAU (appointee to President Reagan's 'Administration of Justice' task force) 1981

A man of sense only trifles with them, plays with them, humours and flatters them, as he does a sprightly forward child; but he neither consults them, nor trusts them with serious matter; though he often makes them believe that he does, which is the thing in the world that they are most proud of.

EARL OF CHESTERFIELD 1694–1773
Letter to his son

I'm not a believer in equality and my attitude is that women are supposed to be pretty and nice. A woman should be a woman.

JIM DAVIDSON 1986

Nature has determined a woman's destiny through beauty, charm, and sweetness. Law and custom may have much to give women that has been withheld from them, but the position of women will surely be what it is: in youth an adored darling and in mature years a loved wife.

SIGMUND FREUD 1856–1939
Letter to his fiancée

She who speaks sweetly to her husband and is a clever manager of household affairs is a true wife. She who is one in spirits with her lord and devotes her whole self to his happiness is a true wife. He whose wife decorates her person with sandal paste, and perfumes her body after daily ablution, talks little and agreeably, partakes small quantities of food, is ever fond of him, and is constantly engaged in doing acts of piety and virtue with a view to bringing happiness and prosperity into the house and is ever ready to yield to the procreative desires of her lord, is not a man but a lord of heaven.

Garuda Purana (Hindu text)

When I have a brand new hair-do,
With my eyelashes all in curl,
I float as the clouds on the air do,
I enjoy being a girl!
When men say I'm cute and funny
And my teeth aren't teeth but pearl,
I just lap it up like honey,
I enjoy being a girl!
I flip when a fellow sends me flowers,
I drool over dresses made of lace,
I talk on the telephone for hours,
With a pound and a half of cream on my face!
I'm strictly a female female,
And my future I hope will be

Nature has determined a woman's destiny

In the home of a brave and free male
Who'll enjoy being a guy having a girl like me.

RODGERS & HAMMERSTEIN
– from *Flower Drum Song* 1958

If we had more feminine women there would be less unemployment, divorce, delinquency and other evils.

ISABELLE STAYT (of the Campaign for the Feminine Woman) 1983

She had this really nice tiny face that I found cute and dinky, that sort of appealed to me. Just the smallness of her face really . . . that you could put your hands around and strangle it.

SIMON
Blind Date TV show 1987

Attractiveness had nothing to do with it. She was a woman. When this certain time comes on me it's a very immediate thing . . . I don't know if I did this – well, for a sex act, or hatred, or for what reason – I think I did this not as a sex act, but out of hate for her – not her in particular, but for a woman.

ALBERT DESALVO ('The Boston Strangler') 1966

Needs a man

Every woman needs a man to discover her.

CHARLIE CHAPLIN 1889–1977

Because women can do nothing except love, they've given it a ridiculous importance.

W. SOMERSET MAUGHAM 1874–1965
Of Human Bondage

Man's love is of man's life a thing apart,
'Tis woman's whole existence.

GEORGE, LORD BYRON 1788–1824
Don Juan

Women don't forget it,
Love is their whole happiness.

WOODS, CAMPBELL & CONNELLY
'Try a Little Tenderness' 1932

To men, love is an incident; to women a vocation. They live by and for their emotions.

DENIS DIDEROT 1713–84
Celibate's Apology

A woman's whole life is a history of the affections.

WASHINGTON IRVING 1783–1859
'The Broken Heart'

You can either choose to love women or to know them. There is no middle way.

French proverb

I'm not sure if a mental relation with a woman doesn't make it impossible to love her. To know the mind of a woman is to end in hating her.

D.H. LAWRENCE 1885–1930
Letter to Dr Trigant Burrow

If women could be fair and yet not fond.

EDWARD DE VERE, EARL OF OXFORD 1550–1604
'Women's Changeableness'

With women the heart argues, not the mind.

MATTHEW ARNOLD 1822–88
Merope

For woman is destined to love, and love comes to women of itself, does not depend upon her free will. But when she loves, it is her duty to marry and the state must not create obstacles to this. Now if a woman holding public office were to marry, two possibilities would follow. First, she might not subject herself to her husband in matters regarding her official duties, which would be utterly against female dignity, for she cannot say then that she has given herself up wholly to her husband. Where are the strict limits that divide official from public life? Or, secondly, she might subject herself utterly to her husband, as nature and morality require. But in that case she would cease to be the official and he would become it. The office would become his by marriage, like the rest of his wife's property and rights.

JOHANN FICHTE 1762–1814
The Science of Rights

By marriage the very being or legal existence of woman is suspended, or at least it is incorporated and consolidated into that of a husband.

SIR WILLIAM BLACKSTONE 1723–80
Commentaries on the Laws of England

Scissors and string, scissors and string,
When a man's single he lives like a king.
Needles and pins, needles and pins,
When a man marries his troubles begin.

Nursery rhyme

He was reputed one of the wise men that made answer to the question when a man should marry? 'A young man, not yet, an elder man not at all.'

FRANCIS BACON 1561–1626
'Of Marriage and Single Life'

The bachelor is a peacock, the engaged man a lion and the married man a jackass.

German proverb

Every woman should marry – and no man.

BENJAMIN DISRAELI 1804–81
Lothair

If we could get on without a wife, Romans, we would all avoid the annoyance, but since nature has ordained that we can neither live very comfortably with them nor at all without them we must take thought for our lasting well-being rather than for the pleasure of the moment.

Q. CAECILIUS METELLUS MACEDONICUS
Speech 131 B.C.

Marriage is a step so grave and decisive that it attracts light-headed, variable men by its very awfulness.

ROBERT LOUIS STEVENSON 1850–94

Before going to war say a prayer,
Before going to sea say two,
Before marrying say three.

Proverb

The attitude towards marriage of the heart-free bachelor must be at best a highly cautious attitude. He knows he is already in the frying-pan (none knows better), but, considering the propinquity of the fire, he doubts whether he had not better stay where he is.

ARNOLD BENNETT 1867–1931
'Marriage'

A wife is a woman who sticks with her husband through all the troubles he wouldn't have had if he hadn't married her!

Cocktail mat

Two days are the best of a man's wedded life:
The days when he marries and buries his wife.

HIPPONAX *c.* 540 B.C.

No man examining his marriage intelligently can fail to observe that it is compounded, at least in part, of slavery, and that he is the slave.

H.L. MENCKEN 1880–1956
'Prejudices'

The natural instinct and ambition of every girl is marriage!

MR JUSTICE GRANTHAM
– quoted in *The Overproduction of Women – and the Remedy*, Mrs Erskine *c.* 1914

Weddings make a lot of people sad,
But if you're not the groom, they're not so bad.

GUS KAHN
'Makin' Whoopee' 1928

A wise man must not take a wife.

THEOPHRASTUS *c.* 372–286 B.C.
On Marriage

He that hath wife and children hath given hostages to fortune; for they are impediments to great enterprise, either of virtue or mischief.

FRANCIS BACON 1561–1626
'Of Marriage and Single Life'

Every woman is a source of annoyance, but she has two good seasons, the one in her bridal chamber and the other in her grave.

PALLADAS early 5th century

About 100,000 women in London alone face danger within their marriage according to official figures . . . One death a month is caused by a husband or lover.

Sunday Mirror 1988

The comfortable estate of widowhood is the hope that keeps up a wife's spirit.

JOHN GAY 1685–1732
The Beggar's Opera

Rich widows are only second-hand goods that sell at first class prices.

BENJAMIN FRANKLIN 1706–90

To the orthodox family of the medieval period a widow was ill-luck incarnate. If young and childless as well, she was all the more calamitous, as a husbandless, barren, menstruating female. Her presence brought contamination, the sound of her voice was a curse, her glance was poisonous, her very existence was perilous and brought ill-luck and woe to all her relations. She was treated as a thing apart for she was already half dead. Her fate has been frequently described. A few days after her husband's death the female relatives invade the widow's house. They push her violently about, make her sit on a stool, cut the thread of her tali (neck ornament), and have a barber shave her head. She is then called by the opprobrious term munda, 'baldie'. This tonsure is repeated as soon as the hair grows a little, since it is believed that a long braid of hair would put the husband in bondage in the next world. From now on she must wear only white clothes. Never again can she wear the sindura mark on the forehead, or jewellery, ornaments or other indications of saubhagya or married bliss. She is forbidden to use a cot, and must sleep on the ground. She cannot cook or help in cooking the family's food; she must eat only once a day and only enough to keep her alive. She is denied even the simple pleasure of chewing pan. She is debarred from all religious affairs and cannot participate in wedding ceremonies or any joyous festivities. Even her son cannot be invited for a sraddha. Shunned by all, even the servants of the household, left in isolation and subjected to scorn and abuse, her possessions, if she had any, coveted by her relations who want her out of the way, it is no wonder that she sometimes chose to end her existence by suttee.

BENJAMIN WALKER
The Hindu World 1968

Be wery careful o' vidders all your life.

CHARLES DICKENS 1812–70
Pickwick Papers

For the crown of our life as it closes
Is darkness, the fruit thereof dust;
No thorns go as deep as a rose's,
And love is more cruel than lust.
Time turns the old days to derision,
Our loves into corpses or wives;
And marriage and death and division
Make barren our lives.

ALGERNON CHARLES SWINBURNE 1837–1909
'Dolores'

A bride must be made to realize that on leaving the tutelage of her family she passes under that of her husband.

NAPOLEON BONAPARTE 1769–1821

The woman who thus surrenders her personality, and yet retains her full dignity in so doing, necessarily gives up to her lover all that she has. For, if she retained the least of her own self, she would thereby confess that it had a higher value for her than her own person; and this undoubtedly would be a lowering of that person. Her own dignity requires that she should give herself up entirely as she is . . . and should utterly lose herself in him. The least consequence is, that she should renounce to him all her property and all her rights. Henceforth she has life and activity only under his eyes and in his business. She has ceased to lead the life of an individual; her life has become a part of the life of her lover. (This is aptly characterized by her assuming his name.)

JOHANN FICHTE 1762–1814
The Science of Rights

Hence while the wife had (herself) no rank, she was held to be of the rank of her husband, and she took her seat according to the position belonging to him.

Kiâo Theh Sǎng (Chinese text)

It is considered that a wife should in general be prepared to make her home in her husband's country.

Home Office statement 1970

With regard to sexual relations, we should note that in giving herself to intercourse, the [unmarried] girl renounces her honour. This is not, however, the case with men, for they have yet another sphere for their ethical activity beyond that of the family.

GEORG HEGEL 1770–1831
The Philosophy of Right

PROPRIETARY RIGHT IN WIFE
The passages cited to the House [of Lords] from Bracton
... Blackstone ... and Holdsworth's History of English
Law ... – and there were no books of higher authority – all
showed that the action which the law gave to the husband
for loss of consortium was founded on the proprietary right
which from ancient times it was considered the husband
had in his wife. It was in fact based on the same ground as
gave a master a right to sue for an injury to his servant if the
latter was thereby unable to perform his duties. It was an
action of trespass for an invasion of the proprietary right
which, arising from the status of villeinage or serfdom, a
master had in his servant.

The Times Law Report 1952

The state by recognizing marriage ... abandons all claims
to consider woman as a legal person. The husband supplies
her place; her marriage utterly annuls her, so far as the state
is concerned, by virtue of her own necessary will, which the
state has guaranteed.

JOHANN FICHTE 1762–1814
The Science of Rights

A woman's income chargeable to tax shall ... [for any
year] during which she is a married woman living with her
husband be deemed for income tax purposes to be his
income and not to be her income.

Income and Corporation Taxes Act 1970

A man ought not to give up work and turn himself into a
mother figure or nanny at the expense of the state. Such a
role is not primarily a male province ... his brain should be
used in work.

JUDGE PAYNE 1979

Needs a man

If a woman nurses a child ... that child becomes an intimate to the following people. First, the woman herself, who is referred to as the milk-mother. Second, the husband of the woman, to whom the milk belongs, referred to as the milk-father.

AYATOLLAH KHOMEINI
A Clarification of Questions 1980

A woman without a husband would always be liable to be sinful.

'Adī Parva', *Mahābhārata* (Hindu text)

It is a sad woman who buys her own perfume.

LENA JAEGER 1955

The body of man makes sense in itself quite apart from that of woman, whereas the latter seems wanting in significance by itself ... Man can think of himself without woman. She cannot think of herself without man.

JULIEN BENDA 1867–1956
Rapport d'Uriel

A woman can't be alone. She needs a man.

MARILYN MONROE 1926–62

Killer Anthony Zitelli, 25, told a New York court he bludgeoned his mother to death to save her from being alone after he left home.

Sunday Mirror 1988

Chin up, ladies, look around the horizon.
Head high, ladies, don't give up the ship.
Look for the silver lining, you gotta go on with the show;
Climb every mountain, to find your Mister Snow.
And always "Hip-Hup" ladies.
There's a brighter tomorrow.
Stiff upper lip up, ladies.
Do or die is the plan.
Don't ever be discouraged, don't ever be perplexed,
There's always another country, Russia may be next!
So keep your chin up, ladies.
Somewhere over the rainbow there's a man.

JERRY HERMAN
– from *Milk and Honey* 1961

Regard the society of women as a necessary unpleasantness of social life, and avoid it as far as possible.

COUNT LEO TOLSTOY 1828–1910

The fair sex is governed by desire. And women care much for pomp and pride ... kings and persons ambitious of lofty stations in life should not be excessively fond of female company.

Agni Purāna (Hindu text)

My name is White, and I don't get along with women. I would rather be at continual odds with women, and am.

E.B. WHITE 1899–1985

We need to be dependent on a man.

MARGUERITE DURAS b. 1914

Be free from women and you are free from care.

ROBERT GOULD
Satire on Wooing 1698

The man who marries always makes the woman a present because she needs marriage and he does not . . . woman is made for man, man is made for life.

HENRI DE MONTHERLANT 1896–1972
Girls

For man and woman, though in one they grow,
Yet, first or last, return again to two.
He to God's image, she to his was made;
So, farther from the fount, the stream at random stray'd.
How could he stand, when, put to double pain,
He must a weaker than himself sustain!
Each might have stood, perhaps; but each alone,
Two wrestlers help to pull each other down.
Not that my verse would blemish all the fair,
But yet if some be bad, 'tis wisdom to beware,
And better shun the bait, than struggle in the snare.

JOHN DRYDEN 1631–1700
'To my honoured kinsman, John Dryden'

Solitary women exhibit pseudo-masculine efficiency, a determined practical competence which they might expect or demand from a husband if only they had one.

ANTHONY STORR
Human Aggression 1968

A lady's imagination is very rapid; it jumps from admiration to love, from love to matrimony, in a moment.

JANE AUSTEN 1775–1817
Price and Prejudice

Are you really
Taking a wife? You used to be sane enough – what
Fury's got into you, what snake has stung you up?
Why endure such bitch-tyranny when rope's available
By the fathom, when all those dizzying top-floor windows
Are open for you, when there are bridges handy
To jump from? Supposing none of these exits catches
Your fancy, isn't it better to sleep with a pretty boy?
Boys don't quarrel all night, or nag you for little presents
While they're on the job, or complain that you don't
    come
Up to their expectations, or demand more gasping
    passion.

JUVENAL *c.* A.D. 55–140
Satires

      Love a woman? You're an ass!
      'Tis a most insipid passion
      To choose out for your happiness
      The silliest part of God's creation.

      Let the porter and the groom,
      Things designed for dirty slaves,
      Drudge in fair Aurelia's womb
      To get supply for age and graves.

      Farewell, woman! I intend
      Henceforth every night to sit
      With my lewd, well-nurtured friend,
      Drinking to engender wit.

      Then give me health, wealth, mirth, and wine,
      And, if busy love entrenches,
      There's a sweet, soft page of mine
      Does the trick worth forty wenches.

JOHN WILMOT, EARL OF ROCHESTER 1647–80

No spectacle on earth more appealing

If all the girls turn Beauty Queens
An' get their dearest wishes –
Who's going to cook the food we eat
An' wash up all the dishes?

Postcard

Stupidity in the kitchen; woman as cook; the terrible
thoughtlessness with which the feeding of the family and
the master of the house is managed! Woman does not
understand what food means; and she insists on being
cook!

F.W. NIETZSCHE 1844–1900
Beyond Good and Evil

A necessary object, woman, who is needed to preserve the
species or to provide food and drink.

ST THOMAS AQUINAS 1225–74

It is a commonplace of observation that a housewife who
actually knows how to cook, or who can make her own
clothes with enough skill to conceal the fact from the most
casual glance, or who is competent to instruct her children
in the elements of morals, learning and hygiene – it is a
platitude that such a woman is very rare indeed, and that

when she is encountered she is not usually esteemed for her general intelligence.

H.L. MENCKEN 1880–1956
'In Defence of Women'

There is no spectacle on earth more appealing than that of a beautiful woman in the act of cooking dinner for someone she loves.

THOMAS WOLFE 1900–38
The Web and the Rock

The superiority in occupational achievement of men over women, even in such female areas as cooking, is overwhelming . . . It seems reasonable to suppose that sex differences are brought about principally by sex chromosomes. But conclusive evidence is lacking.

A—Z Management

Need I waste time in speaking of the art of weaving, and the management of pancakes and preserves, in which womenkind does really appear to be great, and in which the superiority of the other sex is the most laughable thing in the world?

PLATO 427–347 B.C.
Republic

The best couturiers, hairdressers, home designers and cooks are men. I suspect that were it biologically possible men would make better mothers.

IDA ALEXA ROSS WYLIE
'The Little Woman' 1945

Only motherhood

Clap hands, clap hands!
Till father comes home;
For father's got money
But mother's got none.

Nursery rhyme

Any woman who acts in such a way that she cannot give
birth to as many children as she is capable of makes herself
guilty of that many murders, just as with the woman who
tries to injure herself after conception.

ST AUGUSTINE A.D. 354–430

Womanliness means only motherhood;
All love begins and ends there.

ROBERT BROWNING 1812–89
The Inn Album

Question: What's pink and wrinkly and hangs out your
Y-fronts?
Answer: Your mother.

Joke

Thou, while thy babes around thee cling,
Shalt show us how divine a thing
A woman may be made.

WILLIAM WORDSWORTH 1770–1850
'To a Young Lady'

Women, who are, beyond all doubt, the mothers of all
mischief, also nurse that babe to sleep when he is too noisy.

R.D. BLACKMORE 1825–1900
Lorna Doone

Ninety per cent of our problems with children are probably
the result of a mother who has (1) failed to learn how to
really love her man and submit to him, (2) tried to escape
staying at home, or (3) hindered her husband in the
discipline of the children.

Booklet distributed by the Pro-Family Caucus at White
House Conference on Families, late 1970s

Acting Lance-Bombadier Michael Madden, 36, was jailed
for ten years . . . when he was off-duty he regularly abused,
bullied and assaulted girls aged seven to seventeen . . . Mr.
Gerald Lumley, representing the soldier, said, however,
that although he had acted with the 'utmost depravity and
cruelty' his unhappy childhood and domineering mother
may have contributed to it.

Daily Mail 1988

Men are what their mothers made them.

RALPH WALDO EMERSON 1803–82
The Conduct of Life

Own one

A woman is but an animal, and an animal not of the highest order.

EDMUND BURKE 1722–97
Reflections on the Revolution in France

Woman is like three things: a wolf, a fox and a cat.
Wolf, fox and cat are beasts of prey.
Cat seeks, fox waits, wolf rends and tears.

JEAN DE MEUN *c.* 1240–1305
Roman de la Rose

Friends' husbands always bore one: and friends' wives are – well – all women are cats.

HUGH DE SELINCOURT
A Boy's Marriage 1907

Woman, n. – An animal usually living in the vicinity of Man, and having a rudimentary susceptibility to domestication. It is credited by many of the elder zoologists with a certain vestigial docility acquired in a former state of seclusion, but naturalists of the postsusananthony period, having no knowledge of the seclusion, deny the virtue and declare that such as creation's dawn beheld, it roareth now. The species is the most widely distributed of all beasts of prey, infesting all habitable parts of the globe, from Greenland's spicy mountains to India's moral strand. The popular name (wolf-man) is incorrect, for the creature is of the cat kind. The woman is lithe and graceful in its movements, especially the American variety (felis pugnans), is omnivorous, and can be taught not to talk.

AMBROSE BIERCE 1842–1914
The Devil's Dictionary

What female heart can gold despise?
What cat's averse to fish?

THOMAS GRAY 1716–71
'Ode on the Death of a Favourite Cat'

Women and hens are lost by gadding.

Proverb

Women, priests and poultry have never enough.

Proverb

As a jewel of gold in a swine's snout, so is a fair woman which is without discretion.

'Proverbs', *Holy Bible* (Judaeo-Christian text)

Swine, women and bees cannot be turned.

Proverb

Got a dead wife? No big deal.
Got a dead horse? How you squeal.

Franconian saying

Own one

It is said of the horses in the vision, that "their power was in their mouths and in their tails". What is said of horses in the vision, in reality may be said of women.

JONATHAN SWIFT 1667–1745
Thoughts on various subjects

Women, houses and horses are ominous.

al Bukhari (Islamic text)

Find a woman without an excuse, and find a hare without a meuse.

Proverb

A woman's tongue wags like a lamb's tail.

Proverb

Women and sparrows twitter in company.

Proverb

Many women, many words; many geese, many turds.

Proverb

Where there are women and geese, there wants no noise.

Proverb

Three women, three geese, and three frogs make a market.

Proverb

It is no more pity to see a woman weep than to see a goose go barefoot.

Proverb

Women are like elephants to me; I like to look at them, but I wouldn't want to own one.

W.C. FIELDS 1879–1946

Women and elephants never forget an injury.

SAKI 1870–1917
Reginald

As Abe Martin says, women is just like elephants: I like to look at 'em, but I'd sure hate to own one.

WILL RODGERS 1879–1935

As lions are provided with claws and teeth, and elephants and boars with tusks, bulls with horns, and the cuttle fish with its cloud of inky fluid, so Nature has equipped woman, for her defence and protection, with the arts of dissimulation.

ARTUR SCHOPENHAUER 1788–1860
On Women

I hate women as a race ... we are monkeyish, cruel, irresponsible, superficial.

MRS LYNN LINTON 1822–98
The Girl of the Period

I cannot conceive you to be human creatures, but a sort of

species hardly a degree above a monkey; who has more diverting tricks than any of you.

JONATHAN SWIFT 1667–1745
'Letter to a young lady on her marriage'

Women in state affairs are like monkeys in glass-shops.

Proverb

Women are like wasps in their anger.

Proverb

It is proverbial that from a hungry tiger and an affectionate woman there is no escape.

ERNEST BRAMAH 1869–1942
Kai Lung Unrolls his Mat

With women there can be no lasting friendship; hearts of hyenas are the hearts of women.

Rig Veda (Hindu text)

Right wise it was of our Colm [Columba], when founding in Iona his famous sixth century school and colony of monks and scholars, he forbade the bringing in of a cow. "Where comes a cow" the wise man laid down "there follows a woman; and where comes a woman follows trouble".

SEAMUS MACMANUS
Heavy Hangs the Golden Grain 1951

A woman has the form of an angel, the heart of a serpent, and the mind of an ass.

German proverb

When an ass climbs a ladder, we may find wisdom in women.

Proverb

The sagacity of women, like the sagacity of saints, or that of donkeys, is something outside all questions of ordinary cleverness and ambition.

G.K. CHESTERTON 1874–1936
A Handful of Authors

Prayer is to be interrupted if a dog, a donkey or a woman passes too closely by the place of prayer.

Ahmad ibn Hanbal (Islamic text)

A wicked stepfather took his nine-year-old girl to a football match and chained her to a rope like a dog, a court heard yesterday.

She also suffered more than 100 beatings from him in a year.

Daily Mirror 1988

Women and dogs set men about the ears.

Proverb

Own one

You will find that the woman who is really kind to dogs is always one who has failed to inspire sympathy in men.

SIR MAX BEERBOHM 1872–1956
Zuleika Dobson

The dog is possibly the best available vehicle for parents to use in the sex education of their children. Promiscuity and its results for the female dog present a natural opportunity to discuss similar tendencies and problems in the human female.

St Cloud Minnesota Professional Dog Training
Academy brochure 1976

One advertisement was for a magazine called "Woman and Animals". What is that but an invitation to the most disgusting debasement of man and of animals?

MR BEALE (Prosecuting Counsel)
Cambridge 1980

Woman is a violent and uncontrolled animal, and it is useless to let go the reins and then expect her not to kick over the traces. You must keep her on a tight rein ... Women want total freedom or rather – to call things by their names – total licence. If you allow them to achieve complete equality with men, do you think they will be easier to live with? Not at all. Once they have achieved equality, they will be your masters ...

CATO THE ELDER 234–149 B.C.
– quoted in Livy's *History of Rome*

Plaything

He who believes in nothing still needs a girl to believe in him.

EUGEN ROSENSTOCK-HUESSY
– quoted in W.H. Auden *A Certain World*

A fellow needs a girl to sit by his side
At the end of a weary day.
To sit by his side and listen to him talk
And agree with the things he'll say.
A fellow needs a girl to hold in his arms
When the rest of his world goes wrong,
To hold in his arms and know that she believes
That her fellow is wise and strong.

RODGERS & HAMMERSTEIN
– from *Allegro* 1947

God made the woman for the man
And for the good and increase of the world.

ALFRED, LORD TENNYSON 1809–92
'Edwin Morris'

In all languages the words, Wife, Mother, are spoken with reverence, and associated with the highest, holiest functions of woman's earthly life. To man belongs the kingdom of the

head: to woman the empire of the heart! . . . In every pure
and legitimate relation – as daughter, sister, wife, mother –
woman is the direct assistant of individual man.

JAMES MCGRIGOR ALLAN
Woman Suffrage Wrong 1890

In an uncorrupted woman the sexual impulse does not
manifest itself at all, but only love; and this love is the
natural impulse of a woman to satisfy a man.

JOHANN FICHTE 1762–1814
The Science of Rights

The man's desire is for the woman; but the woman's desire
is rarely other than for the desire of the man.

SAMUEL TAYLOR COLERIDGE 1772–1834
Table Talk

The difference between the third and fourth stages is more
clearly shown in women. In the third stage they get their
pleasure chiefly from the little penis that they have on the
outside of their bodies, called the clitoris, and are mostly
interested in having that organ stimulated. In the adult
stage they get their greatest pleasure from the vagina, which
can be used much more effectively to give pleasure to a male
partner.

ERIC BERNE
A Layman's Guide to Psychiatry and Psychoanalysis
1969

Woman is and always has been primarily a plaything.

GEORGE JEAN NATHAN 1882–1958
'Women as Playthings'

In all countries, then, the ideal woman changes, chameleon-
like, to suit the taste of man; and the great doctrine that her
happiness does somewhat depend on his liking is part of the
very foundation of her existence.

Saturday Review 1867

Somethin' made him the way that he is,
Whether he's false or true,
And somethin' gave him the things that are his.
One of those things is you.

So, when he wants your kisses,
You will give them to the lad,
And anywhere he leads you, you will walk.
And any time he needs you, you'll go runnin' there like
　　mad!
You're his girl and he's your feller
And all the rest is 'talk'.

RODGERS & HAMMERSTEIN
'What's the Use of Wond'rin'', from *Carousel* 1945

The whole education of women should be relative to man.
To be pleasing in his sight, to win his respect and love, to be
useful to him, to make themselves loved and honoured by
him, to train him in childhood, to tend him in manhood, to
counsel and console, to make his life pleasant and happy,
these are the duties of woman for all time, and this is what
she should be taught from her infancy. Woman was made
to yield to man and put up with his injustice.

JEAN-JACQUES ROUSSEAU 1712–78
Émile

Potent in the way of ruling men

Suffer women once to arrive at equality with men, and they will from that moment become our superiors.

CATO THE ELDER 234–149 B.C.
Speech in support of the Oppian Law

A woman is a most arrogant and extremely intractable beast; and this problem would be worse if she even understood that she is no less perfect and no less fit to wear breeches than a man.

P. BORGARUCCI
Della contemplatione anatomica sopra tutte le parti del corpo umano 1564

Women, altho' naturally weak, are high and potent in the way of ruling men.

Fo-Sho-Hing-Tsan-King (Buddhist text)

For the female of the species is more deadly than the male.

RUDYARD KIPLING 1865–1936
'The Female of the Species'

Disguise our bondage as we will,
'Tis woman, woman, rules us still.

THOMAS MOORE 1779–1852
'Sovereign Woman'

God created woman only to tame man.

VOLTAIRE 1694–1778
'From Eve On'

Verily the destruction of men is in obeying their women.

Rasulullah (Islamic text)

The female always gets the better of the male by stillness.
Being still, she takes the lower position. Stillness may be
considered a form of abasement.

'Tâo Teh King', *Lao Tse* (Taoist text)

What infuriates a rather esoteric group of women is that
they want to exert power both through men and also in
their own right, and that this is almost impossible.

SIR JOHN NEWSOM
(Chairman of advisory panel on women's education)
1963

One would wish for every girl who is growing up to
womanhood that it might be brought home to her by some
refined and ethically-minded member of her own sex how
insufferable a person woman becomes when, like a spoilt
child, she exploits the indulgence of man; when she pro-
claims that it is his duty to serve her and to share with her
his power and possessions; when she makes an outcry when

he refuses to part with what is his own; and when she insists upon thrusting her society upon men everywhere.

SIR ALMROTH EDWARD WRIGHT 1861–1947
The Unexpurgated Case Against Woman Suffrage

Why, why, why, why do we let these women bleed us to death.

JOHN OSBORNE
Look Back in Anger 1956

Pretty, but still false

A constant woman – the greatest impossibility!

TIRSO DE MOLINA *c.* 1571–1648
El Amor y el Armistad

Falsehood, vain boldness, craftiness, stupidity, impatience, over-greediness, impurity and harshness are the natural qualities of women.

Devī Bhāgavata (Hindu text)

It is rare that after having given the key of her heart, a woman does not change the lock the day after.

CHARLES SAINTE-BEUVE 1804–69

Who to a woman trusts his peace of mind
Trusts a frail bark, with a tempestuous wind.

GEORGE GRANVILLE 1667–1735
The British Enchanters

. . . Seek roses in December – ice in June;
Hope constancy in wind, or corn in chaff;

Pretty, but still false

Believe a woman or an epitaph,
Or any other thing that's false . . .

GEORGE, LORD BYRON 1788–1824
English Bards and Scotch Reviewers

If you are a man who believes in the word of a woman –
believe me if you do it's only because she's beguiled you.

Old saying

O woman! thou wert fashioned to beguile –
So have all ages said, all poets sung.

JEAN INGELOW 1820–97
'Four Bridges'

Women are less able to curb their coquetry than their
passion.

LA ROCHEFOUCAULD 1613–80
Maxims

Woman's love is writ in water!
Woman's faith is traced in sand.

WILLIAM E. AYTOUN 1813–65
Charles Edwards

Woman's faith, and woman's trust –
Write the characters in dust.

SIR WALTER SCOTT 1771–1832
The Betrothed

A woman is fickle,
Like a feather in the wind:
She's always changing her mind.
Whether weeping or laughing,
The face she presents you
May be pretty, but still false.

F.M. PIAVE
'La donna è mobile', from Verdi's *Rigoletto* 1851

Ophelia: 'Tis brief, my lord.
Hamlet: As woman's love.

WILLIAM SHAKESPEARE 1564–1616
Hamlet

Women imitate the instability of lightning, the sharpness
of weapons and the celerity of the eagle, and the wind.

'Aranya-Khanda', *Rāmāyana* (Hindu text)

A woman friend! He that believes that weakness
Steers in a stormy night without a compass.

JOHN FLETCHER 1579–1625
Women Pleased

Never let a woman grieve you,
Jus' 'cause she got you' weddin' ring.
She'll love you and deceive you,
Then she'll take yo' clo'es and leave you,
Cause a woman is a sometime thing,
Yes, a woman is a sometime thing.

DUBOSE HEYWARD
'A Woman Is a Sometime Thing', from *Porgy and Bess*
(music by George Gershwin) 1935

Pretty, but still false

Woman! when I behold thee flippant, vain,
Inconstant, childish, proud, and full of fancies.

JOHN KEATS 1795–1821
'Woman! When I Behold Thee'

If thou beest borne to strange sights,
Things invisible to see,
Ride ten thousand days and nights,
Till age snow white hairs on thee.
Thou, when thou return'st, wilt tell me
All strange wonders that befell thee,
And swear
No where
Lives a woman true and fair.

If thou findst one, let me know:
Such a Pilgrimage were sweet.
Yet do not, I would not go,
Though at next door we might meet,
Though she were true, when you met her,
And last, till you write your letter,
Yet she
Will be
False, ere I come, to two, or three.

JOHN DONNE 1752–1631
'Song'

A fickle thing and changeful is woman always.

VIRGIL 70–19 B.C.
Aeneid

Warped Colin Hill, 29, raped virgin Leanne three times on
her seventeenth birthday to take "revenge" on his unfaith-
ful wife.
   Then he **strangled** his innocent victim, *shot* her and BEAT

her before kicking her half naked bound body to the bottom of a dyke in desolate fen land.

Sun 1987

> Who holds an eel by its tail
> And a woman to her plighted word
> Must admit he has nothing.

Spanish proverb

A monk should not trust women, knowing them to be full of deceit.

Sutrakritanga (Gaina text)

It is well known that women in particular and small boys are liable to be untruthful and invent stories.

JUDGE SUTCLIFFE
Old Bailey 1976

Here's to the love that lies in woman's eyes. And lies and lies and lies.

Toasts for all occasions Lewis C. Henry (ed.)

There is no sincerity like a woman telling a lie.

NORMAN KRASNA
Indiscreet 1958

Women generally speak falsehood.

'Adī Parva', *Mahābhārata* (Hindu text)

Pretty, but still false

In most places women will not endure to have the truth spoken without raising an outcry.

PLATO *c.* 427–347 B.C.
The Laws

Eight months ago, Carabinieri patrolling the streets near Rome's famous and beautiful Piazza Navona found a mass rape in process: its victim was 30-year-old Maria Camminara ... In court, accusations, interrogations, squalid details, insinuations, insults flew: 'All women are liars, it's a known scientific fact,' said the defence at one point.

Evening Standard 1988

There must be some women who are not liars.

W. SOMERSET MAUGHAM
Time Magazine 1960

Purgatory

I stood at the gate of Paradise, and the majority of those who entered it were the poor, the rich being held back, except that those who were to go to Hell were ordered to be sent there. I stood at the gate of Hell and the majority of those who entered it were women.

'Sahih', *Muslim ibn Hajjaj* (Islamic text)

Men are women's playthings;
Women are the devil's.

VICTOR HUGO 1802–85

What means did the devil find out, or what instrument did his own subtlety present him, as fittest and aptest to work his mischief by? Even by the unquiet vanity of the Woman.

SIR WALTER RALEIGH 1552–1618

Women are the whips of Satan.

Arabian proverb

There is no other purgatory but a woman.

FRANCIS BEAUMONT *c.* 1584–1616 & JOHN FLETCHER
1579–1625
The Scornful Lady

The world is greatly troubled by women. They [men] forsooth say, "these are the vessels of happiness". But this leads them to pain, to delusion, to death, to hell, to birth as hell-beings or brute beasts.

Akârânga Sûtra (Gaina text)

What is woman? Hurtful friendship; inescapable punishment; necessary evil; natural temptation; desirable calamity; domestic danger; delightful injury; born an evil; painted with good colour; gate of the devil; road to iniquity.

Reliquiae Antiquae 11th or 12th century

You are a lady; and wherever ladies are is hell.

GEORGE BERNARD SHAW 1856–1950
Don Juan in Hell

When towards the Devil's House we tread,
Woman's a thousand steps ahead.

JOHANN WOLFGANG VON GOETHE 1749–1832
Faust

Woman is a wheedling and secret enemy. And that she is more perilous than a snare does not speak of the snares of hunters, but of devils.

JACOB SPRENGER & HENDRICH KRAMER
Malleus Maleficarum (the indispensable handbook and ultimate authority for the Inquisition) 1489

Woman . . . is a real devil, an enemy of peace, a source of provocation, a cause of disputes, from whom man must hold himself apart if he wishes to taste tranquillity.

PETRARCH 1304–74
Physic against Fortune

Devil Woman

Cliff Richard song title 1975

(She's Got the) Devil in her Heart

Beatles' song title 1963

You look like an angel,
Walk like an angel,
Talk like an angel,
But I got wise –
You're the devil in disguise.

GIANT, BAUM & KAYE
– sung by Elvis Presley 1963

Remain children

Women remain children their whole life long.

ARTUR SCHOPENHAUER 1788–1860
On Women

A woman may make a man's home delightful, and may thus increase his motives for virtuous exertion. She may refine and tranquillize his mind – may turn away his anger, or allay his grief. Where want of congeniality impairs domestic comfort, the fault is generally chargeable on the female side; for it is for woman, not for man, to make the sacrifice, especially in indifferent matters. She must, in a certain degree, be plastic herself, if she would mould others, and this is one reason why very good women are sometimes very uninfluential. They do a great deal, but they yield nothing . . . In everything that women attempt, they should show their consciousness of dependence. There is something so unpleasant in female self-sufficiency, that it not infrequently prejudices instead of persuading. Their sex should ever teach them to be subordinate; and they should remember that, by them, influence is to be obtained, not by assumption, but by a delicate appeal to affection or principle. Women, in this respect, are something like children: the more they show their need of support, the more engaging they are.

MRS JOHN SANDFORD
Woman in her Social and Domestic Character 1837

Women, then, are only children of a larger growth: they have an entertaining tattle, and sometimes wit; but for solid, reasoning good-sense, I never knew in my life one that had it, or who reasoned or acted consequentially for four and twenty hours together.

EARL OF CHESTERFIELD 1694–1773
Letter to his son

She takes just like a woman, yes, she does
She makes love just like a woman, yes, she does
And she aches just like a woman
But she breaks just like a little girl.

BOB DYLAN
'Just Like a Woman' 1966

One section is the not hearing who are also the not seeing – the women and the children.

Dînkard (Zoroastrian text)

Men, however, though very commonly sadistic, are often masochistic as well; and this is because the inferior, or masochistic, position is one which is shared by both sexes in childhood, and from which the woman need never emerge, although the man must do so if he is to become fully masculine.

ANTHONY STORR
Sexual Deviation 1964

The opinion I have of the generality of women – who appear to me as children to whom I would rather give a sugar plum than my time, forms a barrier against matrimony which I rejoice in.

JOHN KEATS 1795–1821
Letter to George and Georgina Keats

*S*hould be seen at night

Young girls should see, hear, and inquire as little as possible.

XENOPHON b. c. 430 B.C.

Let them lower their gaze before the men at whom it is not lawful for them to look, and let them guard their private parts by veiling them, or by bewaring of (or guarding against) fornication. The lowering of glances is presented because the glance is the messenger of fornication.

al Baydawi (Islamic text)

Let him not eat in the company of his wife, nor look at her, while she eats, sneezes, yawns or sits at her ease.

Laws of Manu (Hindu text)

The face of woman is as a burning wind; the voice of woman is the hissing of serpents.

ST BERNARD OF CLAIRVAUX ('The honey-sweet teacher')
1090–1153

Nothing disgraceful is proper for man, who is endowed with reason; much less for woman, to whom it brings shame even to reflect of what nature she is ... By no manner of means are women to be allowed to uncover and exhibit any part of their person, lest both fall – the men by being excited to look, they by drawing on themselves the eyes of men.

CLEMENT OF ALEXANDRIA *c.* A.D. 150–215

And tell the believing women to lower their gaze and be modest, and display of their ornament only that which is apparent, and to draw their veils over their bosoms, and not to reveal their adornment save to their own husbands or fathers or husbands' fathers.

Surah (Islamic text)

The beauty of women is the greatest snare. Or rather, not the beauty of woman, but unchastened gazing.

ST JOHN CHRYSOSTOM ('Golden Mouth') *c.* A.D. 347–407
Homilies

A woman should be seen at night, in the distance, or under an umbrella.

Japanese proverb

*T*alkers

Women are great talkers.

Proverb

Ten kabs of gossip descended to the world; nine were taken by women.

'Kiddushin', *Talmud* (Jewish text)

One tongue is enough for a woman.

Proverb

People who give their letters large bodies but little else live for the present. They enjoy gossip and like being socially involved. They are not over interested in making money. Women tend to write like this.

JANE PATERSON
Know Yourself Through Your Handwriting 1978

Women are fond of talking.

'Berakoth', *Talmud* (Jewish text)

Women's chief weapon is their tongue and they will not let it rust.

French Proverb

There is an iron 'scold's bridle' in Walton church. They used these things in ancient days for curbing women's tongues. They have given up the attempt now. I suppose iron was getting scarce, and nothing else would be strong enough.

JEROME K. JEROME 1859–1927
Three Men in a Boat

How hard it is for women to keep counsel!

WILLIAM SHAKESPEARE 1564–1616
Julius Caesar

A sieve will hold water better than a woman's mouth a secret.

Proverb

Indiscretion, n.: The guilt of women.

AMBROSE BIERCE 1842–1914
The Devil's Dictionary

Secrets with girls, like loaded guns with boys,
Are never valued till they make a noise.

GEORGE CRABBE 1754–1832
'The Maid's Story'

The Wonder! A woman keeps a secret.

SUSANNAH CENTLIVRE *c.* 1667–1723
Play title

A woman's tongue is the last thing about her that dies.

Proverb

The oceans, fools and women

Three things have been difficult to tame: the oceans, fools and women. We may soon be able to tame the ocean; fools and women will take a little longer.

SPIRO AGNEW 1970

Only women and Petty Man are hard to have around the house. If you become close to them, they turn non-compliant. If you keep them at a distance, they turn resentful.

CONFUCIUS 551–479 B.C.

And a woman is only a woman, but a good cigar is a smoke.

RUDYARD KIPLING 1865–1936
'The Betrothed'

A woman without a husband, O King, and a weak creature, and one without friends or relatives, and a glutton, and one dwelling in a disreputable family, and the friend of sinners, and he whose wealth has been dissipated, and he who has no character, and he who has no occupation, and he who has no means. These are the ten despised and condemned in the world, thought shameful, looked down upon, held blameworthy, treated with contumely, not loved . . .

> *The Questions and Puzzles of Milinda the King*
> (Buddhist text)

These three are not to be accepted as a witness: a woman, a young serving boy, and a man slave.

> *Dînâ-î Maînôg-î Khirad* (Zoroastrian text)

In matters of secrecy a woman, a fool, a boy, a covetous man, a meanminded person and he in whom signs of insanity are marked must not be consulted.

> 'Vana Parva', *Mahābhārata* (Hindu text)

No vote can be given by lunatics, idiots, minors, aliens, females, persons convicted of perjury, subornation of perjury, bribery treating or undue influence, or by those tainted of felony or outlawed in a criminal suit.

> SIR WILLIAM BLACKSTONE 1723–80
> *Commentaries on the Laws of England*

> And when a lady's in the case
> You know all other things give place.

> JOHN GAY 1685–1732
> *Fables*

A trial at Bradford Crown Court yesterday was adjourned *sine die* after a barrister had objected because 11 members of the jury were women.

> *The Times* 1980

The very name's a crime

He seldom errs
Who thinks the worst he can of womankind.

JOHN HOME 1722–1808
Douglas

Among all savage beasts none is found so harmful as woman.

ST JOHN CHRYSOSTOM ('Golden Mouth') *c.* A.D. 347–407

And I have found a woman more bitter than death who is the hunter's snare: and her heart is a net, and her hands are bands. He that pleaseth God shall escape from her: but he that is a sinner shall be caught by her.

'Ecclesiasticus', *Holy Bible* (Judaeo-Christian text)

In their creation Manu gave to women a love of bed and seat, and ornament, impure desires, wrath, dishonesty, malice and bad conduct.

Laws of Manu (Hindu text)

Bad conduct is the taint of a woman.

Dhammapada (Buddhist text)

Oh wicked women, wilful, and variable,
Right false, fickle, fell, and frivolous,
Dogged, dispiteful, dour and disavable [deceitful],
Unkind, cruel, curst, and covetous,
Overlight of laitis [manners], unloyal and lecherous,
Turned from truth, and taiclit [entangled) with treachery,
Unfirm of faith, filled with felony.

> Secular lyrics, late 15th century

The monk should avoid women, knowing them to be like a
poisoned thorn.

> *Sutrakritanga* (Gaina text)

The mouth of a woman rains honey; but her heart is like a
jar full of poison. She uses sweet words; but her heart is
keen like a razor. She has an eye constantly fixed on her
own object, on account of which she is submissive to her
husband. Otherwise she is disobedient. Her face is cheerful;
but her mind is unclean.

> 'Prakriti-Khanda', *Brahma-Vaivarta* (Hindu text)

All my life I was having trouble with women . . . I could feel
in my heart that somebody would always have trouble with
them, so I kept writing those blues.

> MUDDY WATERS 1976

The world is full of care, much like unto a bubble;
Women and care, and care and women, and women and
care and trouble.

> REVD NATHANIEL WARD 1578–1652
> *Simple Cobler's Boy*

I have not left behind a trial more injurious to man than woman.

> 'Kitab al-jami as-sahih', *al Bukhari* (Islamic text)

O women! woe to men, traps for their falls,
Still actors in all tragical mischances,
Earth's necessary ills, captivating thralls,
Now murdering with your tongues, now with your
    glances,
Parents of life and love, spoilers of both,
The thieves of hearts, false, do you love or loath!

> ST ROBERT SOUTHWELL *c.* 1561–95
> *St Peter's Complaint*

Woman! the very name's a crime.

> ROBERT GOULD late 17th century
> Toast

Brigands demand your money or your life; women require both.

> SAMUEL BUTLER 1835–1902

Woman, the most dangerous sport of all.

> F.W. NIETZSCHE 1844–1900
> *Thus Spake Zarathustra*

Women are not a hobby – they're a calamity.

> ALEXANDER BRAILOWSKY 1931

A man with a hundred tongues who lived for a century would still not be able to complete the task of describing the vices and defects of a woman.

> *Mahābhārata* (Hindu text)

This pernicious mischief

The woman, who at the return of the month hath her issue of blood, shall be separated seven days. Every one that toucheth her shall be unclean until the evening. And every thing that she sleepeth on, or that she sitteth on in the days of her separation, shall be defiled. He that toucheth her bed shall wash his clothes: and being himself washed with water, shall be unclean until the evening.

Whosoever shall touch any vessel on which she sitteth shall wash his clothes: and himself being washed with water, shall be defiled until the evening.

If a man copulateth with her in the time of her flowers, he shall be unclean seven days: and every bed on which he shall sleep shall be defiled.

The woman that hath an issue of blood many days out of her ordinary time, or that ceaseth not to flow after the monthly courses, as long as she is subject to this disease, shall be unclean, in the same manner as if she were in her flowers . . .

If the blood stop and cease to run, she shall count seven days of her purification: And on the eighth day she shall offer for herself to the priest two turtles, or two young pigeons, at the door of the tabernacle of the testimony: And he shall offer one for sin, and the other for a holocaust, and he shall pray for her before the Lord, and for the issue of her uncleanness.

'Leviticus', *Holy Bible* (Judaeo-Christian text)

Menstruating women carry with them a poison that could kill an infant in its cradle.

ST ALBERT THE GREAT ('Doctor Universalis') *c.* 1206–80
On the Inner Secrets of Women

NYONIN KINZEI – "No women allowed"
It is thought that Buddha reinforced certain indigenous taboos against the blood associated with menstruation and childbirth. The Mountains HIEIZAN, KOYASAN, OMINESAN, ONTAKESAN, all sacred to Shinto or Buddhism, were known for their strict prohibition of women. Fishermen also banned women from their boats, for the boat spirit (FUNDAMA) was thought to be averse to them.

Encyclopaedia of Japan 1983

With the Awa-nkonde, a tribe at the northern end of Lake Nyassa, it is a rule that after her first menstruation a girl must be kept apart, with a few companions of her own sex, in a darkened house ... called 'the house of the Awa-sungu', that is, 'of maidens who have no hearts'.

J.G. FRAZER 1854–1941
The Golden Bough

Oh! Menstruating woman, thou'st a fiend
From whom all nature should be screened!

Old saying

Among all the Dene and most other American tribes, hardly any other being was the object of so much dread as a menstruating woman. As soon as signs of that condition made themselves apparent in a young girl she was carefully segregated from all but female company, and had to live by herself in a small hut away from the gaze of the villagers or of the male members of the roving band. While in that awful state, she had to abstain from touching anything belonging to man, or the spoils of any venison or other animal, lest she would thereby pollute the same, and condemn the hunters to failure, owing to the anger of the game thus slighted.

J.G. FRAZER 1854–1941
The Golden Bough

It is an undoubted fact that meat spoils when touched by menstruating women.

British Medical Journal 1878

Women are also monthly filled full of superfluous humours, and with them the melancholic blood boils; whereof spring vapours, and are carried up, and conveyed through the nostrils and mouth, etc., to the bewitching of whatsoever it meet. For they belch up a certain breath, wherewith they bewitch whomsoever they list. And of all other women, lean, hollow-eyed, old, beetlebrowed women are the most infectious.

REGINALD SCOT *c.* 1538–99
The Discoverie of Witchcraft

When symptoms of puberty appeared on a girl for the first time, the Guranis of Southern Brazil, on the borders of Paraguay, used to sew her up in her hammock, leaving only a small opening in it to allow her to breathe. In this condition, wrapt up and shrouded like a corpse, she was kept for two or three days or so long as the symptoms lasted, and during this time she had to observe a most rigorous fast.

J.G. FRAZER 1854–1941
The Golden Bough

Among the Chinook Indians who inhabited the coast of Washington State, when a chief's daughter attained to puberty she was hidden for five days from the view of the people . . . it was believed that if she were to look at the sky the weather would be bad; that if she picked berries it would rain; and that when she hung her towel of cedar-bark on a spruce tree, the tree withered up at once.

J.G. FRAZER 1854–1941
The Golden Bough

Reading and carrying the Koran and touching any part of the body to the edges or the spaces between the writings of the Koran as well as tinging with henna and the like are acts which are an abomination for a menstruating woman.

AYATOLLAH KHOMEINI
A Clarification of Questions 1980

But nothing could easily be found that is more remarkable than the monthly flux of women. Contact with it turns new wine sour, crops touched by it become barren, grafts die, seeds in gardens are dried up, the fruit of trees falls off, the bright surface of mirrors in which it is merely reflected is dimmed, the edge of steel and the gleam of ivory are dulled, hives of bees die, even bronze and iron are at once seized by rust, and a horrible smell fills the air; to taste it drives dogs mad and infects their bites with an incurable poison. Moreover bitumen, a substance generally sticky and viscous, that at a certain season of the year floats on the surface of the lake of Judea called the Asphalt Pool, adheres to everything touching it, and cannot be drawn asunder except by a thread soaked in the poisonous fluid in question. Even that very tiny creature the ant is said to be sensitive to it, and throws away grains of corn that taste of it and does not touch them again. Not only does this pernicious mischief occur in a woman every month, but it comes in larger quantity every three months; and in some cases it comes more frequently than once a month, just as in certain women it never occurs at all. The latter, however, do not have children, since the substance in question is the material for human generation, as the semen from the males acting like rennet collects this substance within it, which thereupon immediately is inspired with life and endowed with body.

PLINY A.D. 23–79
Natural History

Among the Baganda, in like manner, no menstruous woman might drink milk or come into contact with any milk-vessel; and she might not touch anything that belonged to her husband, nor sit on his mat, nor cook his food. If she touched anything of his at such a time it was deemed equivalent to wishing him dead or to actually working magic for his destruction. Were she to handle any article of his, he would surely fall ill; were she to touch his weapons, he would certainly be killed in the next battle.

J.G. FRAZER 1854–1941
The Golden Bough

Hands sprinkled in ceremonial ablution when a menstruous woman sees them become quite unclean by her look, and even when she looks hastily and does not see the sacred twigs it is the same ... Prepared food which is within three steps of a menstruous woman is polluted by her and food which she delivers up from her morning meal is not fit for the evening meal ... When she touches the bedding or garments of anyone ... so much space is to be washed with bull's urine and water.

Shâyast Lâ-Shâyast (Zoroastrian text)

This pernicious mischief

As the garments which have been touched by a sacred chief kill those who handle them, so do the things which have been touched by a menstruous woman. An Australian black-fellow, who discovered that his wife had lain on his blanket at her menstrual period, killed her and died of terror himself within a fortnight.

J.G. FRAZER 1854–1941
The Golden Bough

In the Solonge district a menstruating woman could not touch the salted pork or approach the newly killed pig. She would cause the salad dressing to spoil, the mayonnaise to curdle, the very flowers in the fields to lose their aroma. In Hungary the menstruating woman was barred from making preserves, sauerkraut, pickles, or 'paradise apples', or from baking bread.

EDWARD SHORTER
A History of Women's Bodies 1982

French chefs will not even make a mayonnaise while a menstruating woman is in the kitchen. "Are you feeling quite well today, Madam?" he will ask before setting his hand to the cuisine.

MARY KENNY 1977

They will ask thee about menstruation. Say "It is a hurt". So keep apart from women in their menstruation, and go not near them till they be cleansed, but when they are cleansed come into them by where God has ordered you.

Koran (Islamic text)

The womb is frequently subject to suffocation. Suffocation is the name doctors give to a constriction of the vital breathing caused by a defect in the womb. This hinders the woman's breathing. It happens whenever the womb moves from its proper place. Then as a result of a chill in the heart, women sometimes swoon, feel weakness in the heart, or suffer dizziness . . .

This illness befalls women when they are full of spoiled and poisonous menstrual blood. It would therefore be good for such women, whoever they be, whether young or old, to have frequent sexual intercourse so as to expel this matter. It is particularly good for young women, as they are full of moisture.

ST ALBERT THE GREAT ('Doctor Universalis') *c.* 1206–80
On the Inner Secrets of Women

Chapter I describes the factors that determine the length of the periods of uncleanness in various classes of women, particularly with reference to the retroactive effect of uncleanness.

Chapter II states the tests which establish the beginning of the menstrual period and indicates which colours of discharge are clean and which are unclean.

Chapter III deals with the woman in childbirth, stating under what condition and for what length of time she is unclean, and determining the period of uncleanness in those cases where the sex of the child cannot be established either because of hermaphroditism or on account of miscarriage or abortion.

Chapter IV is concerned with the condition of uncleanness of non-Jewish women, such as Samaritans, Sadduceans and idolaters and of women in protracted labour.

Chapter V deals with the uncleanness of a woman whose child was delivered by a Caesarian section. It indicates also the signs of puberty in both sexes, determining their symptoms and the times of their appearance.

Chapter VI gives further details on the signs of puberty in the female. (In this connection the rule is evolved that on the appearance of a particular symptom the others are assumed to exist, whereas the converse is not true . . .)

Chapter VII discusses the uncleanness of menstrual blood and other impurities. It also states the circumstances and to what extent Samaritans are believed in regard to uncleanness.

Chapters VIII–X indicate the tests to be applied to decide whether a stain is that of menstrual blood or of some other matter; describe the symptoms of the approach of the menstrual period; and deal finally with the condition of uncleanness of the corpse of a menstruant.

Contents page, 'Niddah', *Talmud* (Jewish text)

If a woman begins menstruating while praying her prayer is void.

AYATOLLAH KHOMEINI
A Clarification of Questions 1980

A man is not permitted to have intercourse with his wife during the menstrual period. If he does so under the influence of lust, expiation becomes binding.

Abu Da'ud (Islamic text)

Whosoever shall lie in sexual intercourse with a woman who has an issue of blood, either out of the ordinary course or at the usual period, does no better deed than if he should burn the corpse of his own son, born of his own body, and killed by a spear, and drop its fat into the fire.

Fargard (Zoroastrian text)

Troubled with evil humours

The cause why women are oftener found to be witches than men: they have such an unbridled force of fury and concupiscence naturally that by no means is it possible for them to temper or moderate the same. So as upon every trifling occasion, they (like brute beasts) fix their furious eyes upon the party whom they bewitch. Hereby it comes to pass that women, having a marvellous fickle nature, when grief so ever happens unto them, immediately all peace-ableness of mind departs; and they are so troubled with evil humours that out go their venomous exhalations, engen-dered through their ill-favoured diet, and increased by means of their pernicious excrements, which they expel.

REGINALD SCOT *c.* 1538–99
The Discoverie of Witchcraft

All witchcraft comes from carnal lust which in women is insatiable.

JACOB SPRENGER & HENDRICH KRAMER
Malleus Maleficarum (handbook of the Inquisition) 1489

A woman is the embodiment of rashness and a mine of vices. She is hypocritical, recalcitrant and treacherous. She is an obstacle to the path of devotion. She is practically a witch and represents vile desire.

'Prakriti-Khanda', *Brahma-Vaivarta* (Hindu text)

For every male witch there are fifty female witches . . . In my opinion this is not due to the weakness of the sex – for most of them are intractably obstinate – it is more likely that they were reduced to this extremity by bestial cupidity . . . For one sees that women's visceral parts are bigger than those of men whose cupidity is less violent. On the other hand, men have bigger heads, and therefore have more brains and sense than women. The poets demonstrated this metaphorically when they said that Pallas Athena, goddess of wisdom, sprang from the brain of Jupiter and had no mother: they meant to show that wisdom cannot come from women, whose nature is nearer to that of brute beasts. I must add – Satan first addressed himself to woman, who then seduced man. I consider that God wanted to weaken and tame Satan by giving him power over the least worthy of creatures, such as snakes, flies and other beasts rather than over men, and over woman rather than over man.

JEAN BODIN *c.* 1530–96
On the Demon-worship of the Sorcerers

When a woman love pretends
'Tis but till she gains her ends,
And for better and for worse
Is for Marrow of the Purse.
Where she jilts you o'er and o'er,
Proves a slattern or a whore,
This hour will tease will tease and vex
And will cuckold you the next;
They were all contrived in spight
To torment us, not delight,
But to scold to scold to scratch and bite,
And not one of them proves right,
But all, all are witches by this light,
And so I fairly bid 'em and the world good night.

Song from *Orpheus Brittanicus*, in the collection
Wit and Mirth 1719

Watch them closely

A woman's place is in the home.

Proverb

A woman who has entered into a permanent marriage is not allowed to leave the house without her husband's permission. She must submit herself to any pleasure he desires. She may not refuse herself on any grounds other than religious ones ... If a woman does not obey her husband according to the manner set out in the previous problems she is then sinful and is not entitled to food, clothes, housing or intercourse.

AYATOLLAH KHOMEINI
A Clarification of Questions 1980

Woman is an empty thing and easily swayed: she runs great risks when she is away from her husband. Therefore, keep females in the house, watch them closely, and return home frequently to keep an eye on your affairs and to keep them in fear and trembling. Make sure they always have work to do in the house and never allow them to be idle, for idleness is a great danger to both man and woman, but more to the woman.

PAOLO DA CERTALDO *c.* 1300–70
Libro di buoni costumi

C. Sulpicius Gallus was another stern and pitiless husband: he repudiated his wife because she had been seen out of doors with her face uncovered. The sentence was harsh but based on reason. 'The law' he could have said to her 'bids you seek to please no one but me. It is for me that you must be attractive. For me that you must adorn yourself. To me you must confide the secrets of your beauty. In sum, I am to be the judge of your charms. Any other glance which you attract to yourself, even innocently, can only render you suspect of entertaining some criminal design.'

VALERIUS MAXIMUS *c.* 10 B.C.–A.D. 50

After all, what does a strict guard avail, as a lewd wife cannot be watched and a chaste one does not have to be?

JOHN OF SALISBURY *c.* 1115–80
Polycraticus

Any woman who goes out of the house without the permission of her husband, then all the angels of the Heavens curse her till she returns, and, besides, men and Jinn [spirits] of whatever object she passes by curse her.

Tabrani (Islamic text)

The husband must possess the absolute power and right to say to his wife: 'Madam, you shall not go out, you shall not go to the theatre, you shall not receive such and such a person; for the children you will bear shall be mine.'

NAPOLEON BONAPARTE 1769–1821

The last girl to fall for the charm of Wilmot Austin hurled herself from a 12th-floor window.

After the death of Linda Ofori, aged 20, a police inquiry revealed Austin, of Penge House, Wye Street, Battersea, had imprisoned one girlfriend after another for six years.

231

Austin made a tape recording of one of the women's screams as he put his hands round her throat. He wrote on the tape "The Killing of Marcia McLean" and played it back to her once she had recovered.

Austin, six foot one inch tall and powerfully built, found it easy to chat up women, the court heard.

At 17 he held his girlfriend, Jennifer Tull, aged 22, from Battersea, captive for two days. He tried to suffocate her with a pillow, the court heard. Then he met Marcia McClean, 21, of Penge House. "I thought I was going to die," she told the court.

He held her captive for a week when she wanted to end the relationship. He beat her, threatened to burn her and locked her in a cupboard. He then tried to strangle her and made the sinister tape, later found by the police.

In 1985 his relationship with neighbour Daphne Wedderburne went sour. She was held captive for 22 hours and slashed her wrist. She was finally released. When Linda Ofori resorted to suicide from Austin's tower-block flat, eyewitnesses said Austin kicked her body and screamed, "What did you do that for, you silly cow."

Streatham and Tooting News 1988

A woman should be good for everything at home, but abroad good for nothing.

EURIPIDES *c.* 484–406 B.C.
Meleager

When the gods made woman

Woman – housewife or harlot?

PIERRE JOSEPH PROUDHON 1809–65

When the gods made woman they made her mind different from man's.

They made her of a bristly sow. Everything about her is messy, defiled with dirt; and she herself gets fat sitting on dunghills in clothes as disgusting as herself. So much for one kind of woman.

Another type the gods made of a wicked vixen. This know-all notices everything, whether it is good or bad. The bad she calls good, and good bad. She's always changing her mind.

They made another from a bitch, a busybody like her mother. She wants to hear all and know all and is always poking her nose into everything. No man can stop her threats, not even if he knocks her teeth out with a stone or speaks kindly to her, even if she is sitting among strangers.

The gods made another from Earth. This one is thick – she can't tell good from evil. All she does is eat, and when it's freezing she hasn't got the wits to put her stool nearer the fire.

Yet another the gods made of the sea. She laughs a lot, and any stranger, seeing her, would say: "This is certainly the best wife in the world, and the prettiest." But the next day she won't let you near her for snapping. The summer sea might be calm and beautiful but without warning it will rage and storm. This kind of woman is exactly like the sea.

One the gods made from a stubborn, decrepit donkey. She does nothing unless threatened, and everything she does is only half-done. However, she eats all day, no matter where she is, and sleeps around a lot.

There is also the woman made from a cat. She is not sweet or sexy. She is always miaowing for a mate, but if she gets one he couldn't be more revolted. She's also extremely unpleasant about her friends.

Then there's the longmaned mare. She won't work at the mill or throw out the rubbish or cook. She takes a husband only when pushed, and is always washing herself, rubbing herself with oils and fiddling with her hair. She looks good to strangers – not to her husband (unless he happens to prefer a wife who's a clothes-horse).

Yet another was made of an ape. She is the worst – foul face, short neck, flabby hips, spindly legs – the gods have pity on her husband! Men snigger as she waddles along the street. But she doesn't care a damn. She hates men anyway . . .

You see, woman is the greatest evil the gods have created. A man who is lumbered with a woman rarely spends a day without misery . . .

SEMONIDES OF AMORGUS *c.* 7th century B.C.
Women

The Geography of Women:
In her teens she is like Africa, virgin and unexplored.
In her twenties she's like Australia, highly developed in the built-up areas.
In her thirties she's like America, adventurous, brash and neat on technique.
In her forties she's like Asia, sultry, hot and mysterious.
In her fifties she's like Europe, devastated but still interesting in places.

In her sixties she's like Antarctica – everyone knows where it is but nobody wants to go there.

Joke

'When a girl is under 21 she is protected by law; when she's over 65 she's protected by nature and anywhere in between she's fair game.'

STANLEY SHAPIRO & MAURICE RICHLIN
Cary Grant in the film *Operation Petticoat* 1959

Ah, that the eugenists would breed a woman as capable of laughter as the girl of twenty and as adept at knowing when not to laugh as the woman of thirty-nine!

H.L. MENCKEN 1880–1956
'Prejudices'

Women are most fascinating between the ages of 35 and 40 after they have won a few races and know how to pace themselves. Since few women ever pass 40, maximum fascination can continue indefinitely.

CHRISTIAN DIOR 1905–57

A good woman inspires a man, a brilliant woman interests him, a beautiful woman fascinates and a sympathetic woman gets him!

Cocktail mat

We have hetaera for pleasure, concubines for the daily care of the body and wives for the production of full-blooded children and reliable guardians for the house.

DEMOSTHENES *c.* 383–322 B.C.

Who is't can read a woman

Women, as they are like riddles in being unintelligible, so generally resemble them in this that they please us no longer when once we know them.

ALEXANDER POPE 1688–1744
Thoughts on Various Subjects

Three mysteries there are too high for me, and a fourth is beyond my ken; eagle that flies in air, viper that crawls on rock, ship that sails the seas, and man that goes courting maid.

'Proverbs', *Holy Bible* (Judaeo-Christian text)

WHY IS A SHIP CALLED SHE?
A ship is called 'she' because there is always a great deal of bustle around her; there is usually a gang of men about, she has a waist and stays; it takes a lot of paint to keep her good looking; it is not the initial expense that breaks you, it is the upkeep; she can be all decked out; it takes an experienced man to handle her correctly; and without a man at the helm, she is absolutely uncontrollable. She shows her topsides, hides her bottom and, when coming into port, always heads for the buoys.

Tea cloth

Who is't can read a woman

A ship and a woman are ever repairing.

Proverb

Who is't can read a woman?

WILLIAM SHAKESPEARE 1564–1616
Cymbeline

'Dealing with a man', said the nightwatchman thoughtfully, 'is as easy as a teetotaller walking along a nice wide pavement; dealing with a woman is like the same teetotaller, after four or five whiskies, trying to get up a step that ain't there.'

W.W. JACOBS 1863–1943
Deep Waters

A woman is a foreign land,
Of which, though there he settle young,
A man will ne'er quite understand
The customs, politics, and tongue.

COVENTRY PATMORE 1823–96
The Angel in the House

Women, even when gifted with understanding, are curious creatures.

KARL MARX 1818–83
Letter to Engels

Mirages are like women – strictly unpredictable. They always look inviting, cool and attractive, but you can't pin one down.

HARRY OLIVER
The Desert Rat Scrap Book

A Misogynist's Source Book

There is no worse evil than a bad woman; and nothing has ever been produced better than a good one.

EURIPIDES *c.* 480–406 B.C.
Melanippe

O Woman! in our hours of ease,
Uncertain, coy, and hard to please,
And variable as the shade
By the light quivering aspen made;
When pain and anguish wring the brow,
A ministering angel thou!

SIR WALTER SCOTT 1771–1832
Marmion

Lost is our freedom
When we submit to women so;
Why do we need them
When in their best they work our woe?

THOMAS CAMPION 1567–1620
Booke of Aires

Well, you can't make women happy, that's a kind of fundamental law of the universe. You try and make them happy and they'll never forgive you for revealing to them that they can't be.

LEN DEIGHTON
Spy Story 1974

The way of women – when you will, they won't:
And when you won't, they're dying for you.

TERENCE 190–159 B.C.
Eunuchus

To be a woman is something so strange, so confused, so complicated, that no one predicate comes near expressing it and that the multiple predicates that one would like to use are so contradictory that only a woman could put up with it.

> SÖREN KIERKEGAARD 1813–55
> *Stages on the Road of Life*

There is a tide in the affairs of women,
Which, taken at the flood, leads – God knows where.

> GEORGE, LORD BYRON 1788–1824
> *Don Juan*

The feeling of identity in all circumstances is quite lacking in the true woman, because her memory, even if exceptionally good, is devoid of continuity ... women, if they look back on their earlier lives, never understand themselves.

> OTTO WEININGER
> *Sex and Character* 1906

When I say that I know women, I mean I know that I don't know them. Every single woman I ever knew is a puzzle to me, as, I have no doubt, she is to herself.

> WILLIAM MAKEPEACE THACKERAY 1811–63
> *Mr Brown's Letters*

Throughout history people have knocked their heads against the riddle of the nature of femininity ... Nor will you have escaped worrying over this problem – those of you who are men; to those of you who are women this will not apply – you are yourselves the problem.

> SIGMUND FREUD 1856–1939

The final word

Women, I warn you, are no longer to be trusted.

HOMER *c.* 850–800 B.C.
The Odyssey

Index

Index

Index

Index

Acknowledgments

I would like to thank Maria Aitken, E. Finlay and J. Allen of Balham Library, Maria Dickey of Battersea Reference Library, Carole Blake, The British Library, the staff of the canteen at the Citizens' Theatre Glasgow, Frances Coady, Dr Eveline Cruickshanks, the *Daily Telegraph* Information Service, David Dougan, Wendy Foulger of the Equal Opportunities Commission, The Fawcett Library, The Fawcett Society, Dee Dee Glass, Sheila Hancock, Petrina Horswill, Celia Imrie, Helena Kennedy, Renos Liondaris, Liverpool University Library, Anna Patrick, Fiona Plowman, Andrew Serkis, Robin Soans, Sian Thomas, Dr Ann Thompson, Dani Tomlin, Jack Vaughan, Derek Watson, Chris Webber, Sarah Westcott, and my mother, Fidelis Morgan sr.

Song lyrics are reproduced by permission of the following: for 'Try a Little Tenderness' (Woods, Campbell & Connelly © 1932) – Campbell, Connelly & Co. Ltd, London w1; for 'Devil in Disguise' (Giant, Baum & Kaye) & 'Hard Headed Woman' (Claude de Metrius) – Carlin Music Corporation, 14 New Burlington Street, London w1x 2LR; for 'Chin Up Ladies' & 'It Takes a Woman' (Jerry Herman) – Chappell Morris; for 'How to Handle a Woman', 'A Hymn to Him' & 'Why Can't a Woman' (Alan Jay Lerner), 'Everybody Ought to Have a Maid' (Stephen Sondheim), 'If a Girl Isn't Pretty' (Bob Merrill), 'When I'm Not Near the Girl I Love' (E. Y. Harburg & Burton Lane) & 'A Woman Is a Sometime Thing' (Dubose Heyward) – Chappell Music Ltd; for 'Wives and Lovers' (Hal David) – Famous Chappell Ltd; for 'Just Like a Woman' (Bob Dylan, © 1966 Dwarf Music USA) – B. Feldman & Co. Ltd, London wc2h oea; for 'Love the One You're With' (Stephen Stills © 1986) – Goldhill Music Inc./BMG Music Publishing Ltd; for 'Living Doll' (Lionel Bart) – Peter Maurice Music Co. Ltd, London wc2h oea; for 'Run For Your Life' (Lennon & McCartney © 1965) – Northern Songs under licence to SBK Songs Ltd, 3–5 Rathbone Place, London w1p 4DA; for 'Makin' Whoopee' (Gus Kahn © 1928) – Keith Prowse Music Publishing Co. Ltd/EMI Music Publishing Ltd, London wc2h oea; for 'Big Mouth Strikes Again' & 'Handsome Devil' (Morrissey), 'If I Was With a Woman' (Ian Dury) & 'A Woman's Touch' (P. F. Webster & Sammy Fain) – Warner Chappell Music Ltd; for 'A Fellow Needs a Girl' & 'I Enjoy Being a Girl' (Richard Rodgers & Oscar Hammerstein II © 1947 & © 1958 respectively, copyright renewed; Williamson Music Co. owns publications & allied rights), & 'What's the Use of Wond'rin'' (Rodgers & Hammerstein, © 1945 Williamson Music Co., copyright renewed) – Williamson Music Co., all rights reserved.